The Av

The Avengers

Toby Miller

 Publishing

First published in 1997 by the
British Film Institute,
21 Stephen St,
London WlP 2LN

Reprinted 1998

The British Film Institute exists to promote appreciation, enjoyment,
protection and development of moving image culture in and throughout
the whole of the United Kingdom. Its activities include the National Film
and Television Archive; the National Film Theatre; the Museum of the
Moving Image; the London Film Festival; the production and distribution
of film and video; funding and support for regional activities; Library and
Information Services; Stills, Posters and Designs; Research; Publishing and
Education; and the monthly *Sight and Sound* magazine.

Cover design: Swerlybird Art & Design
Cover image: Patrick Macnee as John Steed and Diana Rigg as Emma Peel
Designed by Andrew Sutterby
Stills courtesy of BFI Stills, Posters and Designs, and by permission of
Canal+ Image UK Ltd.

Set in Minion by Dorchester Typesetting

Printed in Great Britain by The Bath Press, Bath

British Library Cataloguing-in-Publication Data
A catalogue record for this book is available from the British Library
ISBN 0-85170-558-8 pbk

Contents

Acknowledgments

This project has been a wonderful experience. The problems of writing a short history of a decade-long TV series were subordinated again and again to the pleasure of the exercise. This is a tribute to the programme itself and to the many individuals who enabled me to learn about it. Sincere thanks are due to: Jo Barnes, jbenn, Alex Bennett, Sarah Berry, Sue Bobbermein, William Boddy, Rachael Bosley, Sarah Boston, Paola Brandolisio, Scott Bukatman, Ed Buscombe, Jessie Buscombe, Charlotte Butzin, Margaret Cohen, Jeff Coulter, Stuart Cunningham, Michael Curtin, James Dawe, Bryony Dixon, Faye Ginsburg, Ann Harris, Franklin Harris, John Hartley, Tobin Heminway, Bev Hooper, Lisa Howard, Gareth Humphreys, Ian Hunter, Piers Johnson, Keith of Lord Thomas Design, Noel King, Niall Lucy, Catharine Lumby, Anne McClintock, Alex McHoul, Anthony McKay, Denise McKenna, Tony May, Tony Mechele, Eric Monder, Erika Muhammad, Ian Mundwyler, Alondra Nelson, Rob Nixon, Tom O'Regan, Alexis Pasqua, Dana Polan, Andrew Ross, Dorle Ruthrof, Claudia Schwarz, Rita Shanahan, Ella Shohat, Bill Simon, Ron Simon, Hazel Speed, Bob Stam, Grant Stone, Jon Stratton, Alison Strauss, Tim Taylor, Steve Tollervey, Florent Toniello, Graeme Turner, Tise Vahimagi, Ken Wark, Colin White, Rob White, and all the staff of the National Film and Television Archive and the BFI who assisted in the production of this volume. Special thanks are due to those who read the manuscript: Sarah Be, William, Ed, and Dana. Without the example of Ed Buscombe, the best kind of screen intellectual, this book would not have been written.
The result is dedicated to Doreen Price, for taking me to spy films on half-holidays in 1965.

Introduction

It's impossible to watch this stupidity, this excellent
stupidity, this silly excellence without being struck by
black thoughts about design and vision, about content and
vision, about content and about form. You see, it is made
brilliantly. . . . *The Avengers* is excited surface—Harry
Craig, BBC Radio, 1963 (quoted in Buxton 98).

The wonderfully good-chap sexuality of it all—the *Times*,
1966 (quoted in 'Good-Chap Sexuality').

Mrs Gale: You know, it's an ironic theory of yours, that
arming for World War III is the sole security against it.
Steed: So long as the arms race goes neck and neck.
Mrs Gale: I don't think anyone would dare start another
war and risk the reprisal.
Steed: Someone will certainly try. History's full of people
who've tried to get away with it.
Mrs Gale: We can't go on arming forever.
Steed: Biscuit?
Mrs Gale: No, thanks—'The Nutshell', 1963.

'I love *The Avengers*' is an unstable remark. What does it refer to?
That question comes up, of course, with a great many screen texts:
when people are talking about *Olympia*, *October*, or a *Ma and Pa
Kettle* film, are they discussing identical versions? For television the
problem is something else again, especially with long-running
drama series composed of core characters that change with the seasons, recurring story-lines, varieties in transmission text across
countries, and a poor archival apparatus. Perhaps 15 per cent of
British TV programmes from the 1960s survive today in any form.
And how could you authenticate the 'real' text? If you viewed *The*

Avengers in the south of England during the 1960s, you may not have seen the first season, which starred Ian Hendry and Patrick Macnee, until an omnibus *Best of the Avengers* in 1964. You would certainly have been unable to watch it on election night that year: ITV cancelled the programme because Honor Blackman had appeared in a commercial for the Liberal Party. But you could have seen her climbing aboard a private plane with Jeremy Thorpe (Pronay; Briggs 447; Teranko 88). If you were a resident of Bunbury in Western Australia in 1965, like my informant Grant, not even 120-foot aerials could guarantee picture reception each week, because there was no repeater station to boost the signal from Perth; many *Avengers* episodes could be heard but not seen. In the days before television came to South Africa, you might have listened to radio adaptations of the series there.

If you followed the series in the United States, you may not have seen Hendry or his successor Blackman at all, until a retrospective in the 1990s; but that was restricted to cable. If you watched in France, you were tuned to *Chapeau Melon et Bottes de Cuir (Bowler Hat and Leather Boots)* and may now be a member of Rue Firmin Gémier's 'Steed & Co.' fan club; in Germany, the programme was called *Mit Schirm, Charm und Melone* (*With Umbrella, Charm and Bowler Hat* – there is an active fan club of the same name), and *De Wrekers* in Holland. You'd have followed it by subtitle in Cairo, while Italian viewers tuned in to *Agente Speciale*. If you saw *The Avengers in Color* (named and spelt as such for US sales) in Britain or Australia in 1967, you watched it in black and white with a lack of contrast, because soft-graduation printing stock was unsuited to monochrome. Channel Four's archival 1993 season included early episodes that had been bizarrely edited 30 years earlier to fit the varying interests of franchises across the country (Hume 8; Porter 38).

If you followed *The New Avengers* in the late 1970s, you did so with many episodes shot in Canada and France, because of its status as an international co-production. In 1995, you could have seen it commercial-free and struck from original negatives via Bravo's satellite service in the UK, promoted as 'timewarp television'. If you rented *The Avengers* or *The New Avengers* on video from my local store in 1996, you found them in the science-fiction section. (Perhaps not too much should be made of this. My local bookshop stocks the complete Ayn Rand under cultural studies. Then again . . .) If your bedroom wall, scrapbook, or computer contained images of Diana Rigg and Macnee in the 1990s, they may have come from an old *TV Times* or *Avengers Annual*, a Jubilee video release slick, or World Wide Web addresses in Alberta, Sydney, Glasgow, Maintal, and Lille. A Web site in Surrey did the same for *The New Avengers*. Perhaps you owned commemorative items from a mail-order firm selling *Avengers* T-shirts and trading cards through its home page. (In the 1960s, you could have written to a fanzine artist in Arizona for wax Emma Peel seals.) If you visited the original shooting locations, this was probably via the *Avengerland* guide, or perhaps a 1995 *Avengers Walking Tour*. Then again, you may have read about plans for an *Avengers Studio Kafe* to open in the West End that year, with waiters in bowler hats or mini-skirts and a share of the profits to go to hungry children. If you found out from the Web that Rigg was created a Dame Commander of the British Empire in 1994, that probably came courtesy of WGBH Boston, promoting her *Mystery* omnibus series of British crime TV. Or if you knew how she looked as an Avenger, but not her name or even the series itself, that may have been because you were one of the many young women playing *Comix Zone*, an electronic game featuring Alissa Cyan, a strong female character who closely resembles Emma Peel. If your first encounter with *The Avengers* was via a defence of it as high romanticism, then that *did* happen in Ayn Rand's cultural studies. And if you thought of Rigg in her Peel phase as the ideal person to play Théophile Gautier's *Mademoiselle de Maupin*, you may have read the idea first in the work of Camille Paglia. Conversely, Raymond Williams told you 'a petrol commercial' came to mind as he watched the series, and Julie Burchill thought Mrs Peel 'a girl who'd break your back as soon as . . . [a] Sex Doll would scratch it' (Patrick; Schultz 15; McKay and McKay; Bassom 64; Malitz; Rand 135; Paglia 416–17; R. Williams 42; Burchill 86).

You might have heard of the show in Susan Brownmiller's 1970 lament for Mrs Peel as the one 'heroic woman' on television of her day. Leafing through Lee Tulloch's late 80s novel of New York clubbing, you would have encountered narrator Reality Tuttle's desire 'to borrow Emma Peel's lipstick'; she has 'real respect for a woman who can karate-chop half a dozen men without getting her lip gloss all over the furniture'. If you had been with Oliver Sacks doing his 1996 hospital rounds, you may have looked on as he listened to post-encephalitic patients discussing minute details of the programme as if it had aired only minutes before (Brownmiller, quoted in Efron 8; Tulloch 60; Johnson). Alternatively (outside the ward, no doubt) grunge band Dishwalla's 1995 track 'Miss Emma Peel' may have been playing: 'Miss Emma Peel, black boots can crawl on his face/One last look at the grace of Miss Emma Peel/Catch the curve of your leather heel before he blacks out/That's another one down for Miss Emma Peel'.

You might own some of the 17 *Avengers* novels (several recently repackaged in French), two of them co-written by Macnee, or recall the various music themes from compilation albums or Laurie Johnson's *Avengers* and *New Avengers* suites of 1980, or M. Beat's 1994 sampling of the latter on 'Surrender'. You might also have heard the successful 1963 'Kinky Boots' single by Blackman and Macnee, or been one of the few who attended the unsuccessful 1971 stage play. The mid-70s saw a commercial for Timex watches with Macnee acting the part of Steed, another chance to experience references to the programme. When the British group Wider Television Access commenced retrospective screenings in the early 1980s, *The Avengers* was its most popular series, so you could have encountered it there, through TV spots for deodorant and fresh-breath capsules using footage from the series, by unearthing old Corgi models of *Avengers* cars, jigsaw puzzles, a 'John Steed Swordstick' or the 'Emma Peel Doll'. In 1990, a new novel, written by John Peel and Dave Rogers and with a foreword by Macnee, was published. Timed to commemorate the thirtieth anniversary of the series, it brought all the principal characters together. Neil Gaiman's comic *Steed and Mrs Peel* may also have passed by. Then there was the popular commercial for Sterling Automobiles, with James Bond theme music playing, that finds Macnee addressing the viewer: 'I suppose you were expecting someone else.' And Channel Four screened Paul Madden and Dean Stockton's *Without Walls* documentary about the series in 1992. The much-trumpeted 'All-Star, All-Time TV Hall of Fame' *Vanity Fair* issue of December 1995 might have alerted you to the series. A '42-page Portfolio' contained references to just two imported programmes outside its 'Best of British TV' column. *The Avengers* was one of them. And Macnee reprised his character for the Oasis 1996 video single, 'Don't Look Back in Anger'.

All this dispersal aside, could you be sure that you were one of the *cognoscenti* who really 'got' the show anyhow? Before the series was sold to North America, *TV Guide* critic Robert Musel explained to his 1964 US readers that '*The Avengers* was conceived as a satire of counterespionage thrillers, but the British public still insists on taking it seriously.' Even though more and more viewers were learning that the show was 'tongue in cheek, . . . not quite enough' knew what he did about its true meaning ('Violence' 13).

No wonder there was confusion. An entire ethos of life is on display in *The Avengers* that is alternately satirical, commercial, and self-parodic. Pop art, fashion, tradition, modernity, high Englishness, feminism, espionage, police work, the Cold War, Empire, comic-strip fighting, sadism, fetishism and the fun of the commodity are all present. The series has been censored by British and US networks for perverse sex, censured by Congress for undue violence, banned in England for electoral interference, adored by lesbian viewers for leathery femininity, and reprised in every conceivable form of repertory television. It is still claimed as 'the highest grossing British television export ever', with sales to 120 countries (Frensham; 'French'). The life of any internationally popular TV series is a passage across space and time, a life remade over and over again by discourses, institutions, practices of production, distribution and reception, and the shifts in tempo and context that characterise cultural commodities. Cult TV texts are transformed from broadcast programming into the property of varied and productive publics.

To give some sense to this chaos, I have looked to Roger Chartier's work on the history of the book. He aims to reconstruct 'the diversity of older readings from their sparse and multiple traces', identifying 'the strategies by which authors and publishers tried to impose an orthodoxy or a prescribed reading on the text'. This is, then, a focus on 'the text itself, the object that conveys it, and the act that grasps it'. Chartier's tripartite system looks at how meaning is created in the interstices, the interaction, and the independent functioning of each part: how layout, packaging, illustrations and technology shift, determining the frames available for interpretation, especially as stories are remade and remodelled by these generic and industrial constraints and openings and by readers themselves (157, 161–3, 166). In keeping with this model, I have divided the chapters to come between a basic industrial history, key themes from *The Avengers* episodes (pop, fashion, sex, genre, and the postmodern) and the series' following. I hope that this little book manages to demonstrate how the multifaceted ethos of the programme worked; in short, why so many people found fun in it.

1 *History*

I was the woman and she was the man—Patrick Macnee, Channel Four UK, 1993.

For me it all goes back to a night in March of 1966. I am 14 years old, with hormones so raging that I know by heart the sex scenes in all the James Bond books. Flashing across our RCA black and white set is *the most attractive woman in the world* . . . and she's deftly hurling bad guys over her shoulder while trading quips with some guy in a bowler hat . . . *and she's dressed all in leather!—Daily News*, 1987 (Cosgrove).

At lunchtime, Cantonese [garment] workers watch television reruns of *The Avengers*, with Diana Rigg in beige Nehru jacket and bell-bottoms, coolly talking her way out of danger in Cantonese—*New York Times*, 1990 (Hochswender).

Police Surgeon was a 1960 ITV drama series featuring Ian Hendry as Dr Geoffrey Brent. Although the programme disappointed its producers, Hendry emerged as a star. Sydney Newman, a drama executive at ABC who had learnt Griersonian documentary style in Canada, decided to retain Hendry's character in a new format for 1961, famously pronouncing, 'Let's call it *The Avengers*. I don't know what the fuck it means but it's a good title.' The avenging took place following the murder of a renamed (and privatised) Dr David Keel's fiancée; he joined a mysterious figure named John Steed (Macnee) to fight organised crime. They were contracted for six episodes, which ultimately became 161 *Avengers* programmes plus 26 of the *New Avengers*. Hendry left after a year in search of a film career. His replacement for 1962 was initially conceived as a male role, but Blackman became what she termed 'the first feminist to come into a television serial; the first woman to fight back'

John Steed (Patrick Macnee) and Catherine Gale (Honor Blackman)

'Fog' finds Tara King (Linda Thorson) solving the Gaslight Ghoul murders, copycat crimes from 1888

(Newman, quoted in Sutcliffe 29; Blackman, quoted in Buxton 100).

Other occasional helpers in the early years included Martin Rollason as Dr John King and Julie Stevens as Venus Smith. In later seasons, Steed sometimes had an on-screen superior: Douglas Muir as One-Ten, Paul Whitsun-Jones as Charles, Ronald Radd as Quilpie, and Patrick Newell as Mother (the latter across the final season). But Blackman's Catherine Gale (1962–4) and Diana Rigg's Emma Peel (1965–7) were such strong personalities that the others had no place. The last lead was Linda Thorson as Tara King in 1968, hired on John Huston's recommendation. Much of the show's popularity derived from its strong cast of ensemble players, a number of whom went on to greater fame. (We can commence the list with Charlotte Rampling and Donald Sutherland.) When the programme was cancelled in 1969, it had lasted the duration of the 1960s. Macnee was disappointed but tired after 'eight years of working in what had now become a factory': 30 bowler hats and 19 gallons of champagne had been used. The follow-up *New Avengers* of 1976–7 starred Joanna Lumley as Purdey and Gareth Hunt as Mike Gambit alongside the perennial Macnee (who refers to it today as 'an extremely bad retread of *Kojak*') (Hirshorn 16; 'Peter' 24; Thorson 18; Macnee and Cameron 245, 252; Macnee, quoted in Biederman 27). Most of what follows concentrates on Blackman, Rigg, and him.

The Avengers grew in popularity on the British market over the 1960s, spending 103 weeks in the Top Twenty series between 1961 and 1969. In 1967, it was the third most-watched programme and on the chart for 23 weeks. By that point, the lead actors were learning 60 pages of dialogue a week and working 14-hour days, with about three takes per scene. Ten days of principal photography were allocated to each episode, with an average cost of £30,000. Macnee was paid £100 an episode, rising to £125 or £150 (depending on the version you read) after industrial action and remaining at that level for some time until it was increased to £300 a week and then £600 in 1969. Rigg received £100 a show during most of her run. This was said to have trebled once she broke the unwritten law of publicising her remuneration. As Macnee put it when the series was in syndication across the USA in the early 1990s, 'I earned more money in the last two months on the A&E [Arts and Entertainment cable network] repeats than I earned in the whole nine years of the show! Oh, they were robbers!' In the 1990s, the series remained the most profitable British television export of all time. TV entrepreneur Lew Grade was said to have made £70 million from it. Looking back on the original show during *The New Avengers*, Joan Bakewell observed that the 'colourful, well-set, lavish locations' of 1976 palled beside the early days, when 'the excitement lay . . . in the thrills and spills of television itself', and the very stylistics of the medium were emerging (Gambaccini and Taylor 32; Youlden 61; Houldsworth 37; Mansfield 24; Macnee and Cameron 245; Morley 66; Macnee, quoted in S. Williams; Kelly; de Bono; Bakewell 723). What were those times like?

The Avengers' early life was in marked contrast to equivalent programmes on the schedule, notably the BBC's *Z Cars*, perhaps the most famous police series in British history. A social-realist text that involved extensive community research, *Z Cars'* gritty northern images drew immediate opprobrium from the chief constable of Lancashire, who expressed concern at the representation of his staff in episode 1 of January 1962. It is hard to imagine the chief consta-

Emma Peel (Diana Rigg) débuts in 'The Town of No Return'

ble being similarly troubled by *The Avengers* (even though its first season with Hendry and Macnee had programmes like 'The Frighteners', with conferences in the back of London taxicabs that bespoke an East End network of informants akin to *Callan*'s intelligence sources from the 70s, and a Steed who resembled the anti-hero spivs from post-war British *noir*). There was a far-fetched quality to the scripts. Perhaps this is why *Avengers* episodes from the kinned and video-taped era (before the advent of Mrs Peel in 1965) seem inordinately wordy: that was the only means of building up ironic, multiple diegeses, a fantasy world that could not be generated through montage, *mise en scène* or location action.

Longish takes and minimal editing gave the sense of a staged drama, added to by John Dankworth's haunting jazz score.

As an early scriptwriter put it, style overdetermined content in those days, and authorship was difficult to attribute. Conferences saw Hendry tearing up scripts and rewriting them with Macnee and directors Don Leaver and Peter Hammond. Macnee reminisces of the days when he and Hendry would halve bottles of Scotch in front of kinescoped episodes, conducting rigorous evaluations. Bizarre shooting styles carried the day. The look of the 1961 series drew from a number of influences, turning financial and technical limitations into conceits: *noir*-like points of view through stairwells were preferred to wide-angle establishing shots because of the need to save money on set design. Each programme had ten days for rehearsal and two for production, with just three cameras, as per a sitcom. Occasionally errors of dialogue delivery or shot focus went to air. Executive producer and scriptwriter Brian Clemens was quoted in Channel Four's 1992 retrospective *TV Heaven 1963* on the absence of extras: 'If you were in shot, you were in the plot.' The actors raced from stage to stage to film successive scenes. Blackman recalls 'perspiring, or glowing, or whatever women are supposed to do'. Production protocols allowed for three scripts out of twenty-six to be written off, an astonishingly tight ratio (Howarth and Lyons 35). In the early days of shooting on tape or broadcasting live to air, directors were confronted with scripts that called for ten sets and producers who paid for two, with the remainder to be evoked. Their way of dealing with such circumstances was to generate an omniscient, hyperverbalised narration and to deploy objects and shadows to produce an effect, with German expressionist filmmakers such as Fritz Lang an inspiration, and earlier experience in Hammer movies a rehearsal via the sadistic but cartoonish excessiveness of 1950s British horror. Robert Day and Sidney Hayers, directors of *Corridors of Blood* (1957) and *Circus of Horrors* (1959) respectively, were regulars on the series, and producer Julian Wintle had worked on *Corridors*. (Hayers redeployed Hammer imagery for later 'Cybernauts' episodes. In the first reprise, Peter Cushing was an additional link to the evil science and perversity of Sadian cinema.)

Z Cars, on the other hand, borrowed radio's 'story documentary'

Writer and executive producer Brian Clemens

Patrick Macnee in British upper-class uniform

methods: naturalistic writing and acting. Police work was a device for depicting social relations. We can see the difference between these approaches through an anecdote. One of *Z Cars'* writers, Troy Kennedy Martin, was commissioned later in the 60s, along with his brother Ian, to script a new series. They pulled out of the project under the threat of high production values. Key lighting, colour film stock, and daytime shooting, when put together with two regular heroes, were thought to place gritty realism at risk: some contrast with *The Avengers* team, who longed for such luxuries and the grail of New York sales (Stern 3; Fiddy 'In' 13; Sutcliffe 29; Macpherson; Porter 39; Worpole 47; Laing 125–7).

We should not go wild, however, with handy divisions between domestic social realism and mid-Atlantic fantasy. Newman had joined Britain's ABC network in 1958 to produce *Armchair Theatre*. He created *The Avengers* before moving across to the BBC, where he presided over *Doctor Who* and *Z Cars*, later going back go Canada and attacking the National Film Board for 'stinking with probity!' And Howard Thomas, ABC's chief executive, says Newman was crucial to the move away from social-realist one-off drama that had been the company's *forte*, deeming *The Thin Man* (1934) a nice model of elegant knowingness. But for Clemens, the 'first *Avengers* were very much poor man's *Z Cars*' (Howkins 64; Tankel 85; Newman, quoted in Collins 213; Clemens, quoted in Sutcliffe 29).

It *is* significant that nobody revisited *Z Cars* with a view to US sales, but *The Avengers* was a palimpsest for decades, as devotees of *The Protectors, The Persuaders,* and *Dempsey and Makepeace* can avow. If *Z Cars* embodies the welfare-state reformism of post-war Britain, the brief and fragile consensus now blamed for all manner of economic ills, then *The Avengers* stands for the commodity culture of youth pleasure and the modern moment, when affluence would effortlessly continue and develop. While the post-war Attlee Labour Government's form of life seemed to inhabit the self-consciously northern regionalism of BBC policing, Harold Wilson's combination of white-hot technological modernisation with contemporary popular culture informed ITV espionage's unselfconsciously southern urbanism. As the *Financial Times* put it, '[n]o constables dealing with menopausal shoplifters here'. Perhaps *Z Cars* lives on in the remnants of the National Health Service, with *The Avengers* remodelled in Thatcherite self-aggrandisement: the highly embroidered, psychologised novels written as companions to the series express an alarming hostility to the welfare state, government workers, and trade unionism (despite Andy East's careful delineation of ideological and stylistic differences between their various authors). But when Raymond Williams was engaging in a cultural–materialist analysis of *The Avengers* as television critic for *The Listener* in 1968, he found it difficult to measure against *Z Cars'* successor, *Softly Softly* (you could watch Steed followed by Barlow on Thursday evenings). Although Williams was rather disdainful of 'the British upper-class uniform of bowler hat and umbrella', at least the hyperreal sensibility of the series alerted viewers to the fact that it was 'all game'. The 'wholly demotic style' of *Softly Softly*, by contrast, made the characteristic claims of naturalism, where the ordinariness and fatigue of police life ratify the crime squad's view of the world as 'the only available honest way' of perceiving it. The worker must complain but carry on, the stark realism of the programme offering few alternative readings (Erickson 191–2; Dunkley; Laumer 8–9; East 70–4, 121–2, 178–82; R. Williams 41–2).

Unlike its public broadcasting other, *The Avengers* was not seen on a unified grid. At the beginning of the 1960s, British commercial TV was a weekend regional bazaar. ATV provided programming for London, and ABC, which produced *The Avengers*, was responsible for the north and the midlands. They competed for series and haggled over payments in exchange for each other's material. Because Grade controlled London, he was able to refuse to screen *The Avengers* for some time; unlike the apparently peripheral politics of *Z Cars*, this hyper-sophistication was marked initially as for regional tastes only! Its time slots indicate the target audience; depending on the region, the programme was screened between 9.50 and 10.25 on Saturday nights, or 10.41 on Sunday evenings. Blackman and Macnee were voted 'Independent Television's Personalities of 1963' at the Variety Club of Great Britain, and, as has been noted, their early work was packaged as *The Best of the Avengers* and networked across Britain in 1964. By that year, the show claimed ten million regular viewers. Its popularity aggravated some. In 1963 the BBC cancelled *That Was the Week That Was*, its sharp programme of political satire, to great controversy. A general election was imminent, and the series was said to have adopted an anti-Tory stance. The alternative claim, made by ITV, was that Steed and Mrs Gale had denuded the show of its audience. This led in turn to a BBC spokesperson referring to *The Avengers* as a 'malodorous farmyard' (Donaldson 'Gilded'; Rogers *Complete* 61; Alsop 16; Gowers; BBC, quoted in Briggs 374).

Far from being rustic, *The Avengers* was a landmark in the new international division of cultural labour. Macnee as well as Newman was bought from Canada, where Blackman had also worked for a number of years, Rigg had done radio drama, Thorson was growing up, and producer Leonard White had acted. Roger Marshall, writer of many episodes, had learnt his craft in Hollywood working on *Sea Hunt* and *Markham*. He also wrote scripts for *Danger Man* and went on later to *The Sweeney* and *The Professionals*. All sold overseas. Other personnel were key players in later screen landmarks: Gil Taylor lit *Repulsion* (1965) and *Star Wars* (1977), John Moxey directed *Charlie's Angels*, Charles Crichton directed and co-wrote *A Fish Called Wanda* (1988), Alan Hume shot several Bond pictures and *Shirley Valentine* (1989), and Robert Fuest directed *Wuthering Heights* (1970) (Donaldson 'Gilded'; Macnee and Cameron 169; Stern; Sweeting).

By late 1963, there were suggestions of a stage musical to be produced by Cheryl Crawford and a movie made by Halas Batchelor Cartoon Films with Louis de Rochemont. But then the programme itself was interrupted. Blackman had wanted the series made on film, and tried to use her popularity to push for this in return for *not* taking the role of Pussy Galore in *Goldfinger* (1964), but the producers refused and she left. Macnee was furious with her for putting the show at risk. But then Associated British Pathé, which owned ABC, was persuaded to pour £1 million into shooting on film in 1965. The Blackman episodes had been shown in Australia, Italy and Canada. Moving to film was a prerequisite to sales in the USA. There was an intensive and much-publicised search for a new female lead. Elizabeth Shepherd was selected, and some shooting done before she was rejected as unsuitable. Rigg caught the producers' eye in *Armchair Theatre* and was chosen instead. Clemens's influence grew and he contracted Philip Levene, who wrote the noted science-fiction episodes 'The Man-Eater of Surrey Green' and 'The Cybernauts'; Dennis Spooner of *Doctor Who* fame also arrived on the scene. To economise, several scripts from the Blackman days were rewritten for Rigg (Youlden 57; Fakrikian 'Projects' 18; Banks-Smith 'Cathy's'; Macnee and Cameron 234, 237; Maurice Richardson, 3 October 1965 and 'On').

Rejected by NBC and CBS, the series was bought by ABC, which lacked a home-grown espionage show. It was the last black-and-white programme purchased by the networks. The sale netted US $2 million for the first 26 episodes, with US $4.5 million for additional options, reportedly exceeding profits for any British entertainment export apart from The Beatles. In New York terms the cost represented 'incidental monies'. It was initially screened at 7.30

on Saturday nights, not a profitable hour, and then was held in reserve to replace mid-season failures. Part of the impetus to import may have come from profit sueezes experienced by US networks in the 60s. They cut the number of episodes commissioned for new series by half, but were anxious that a surfeit of reruns would alienate audiences (Shapiro 106–7, 120–1, 304–5, 318–19, 404–5, 420–1, 510–11, 526–7; Schultz 5; 'The Avengers'; Papazian 54).

The Avengers ran in the US spring of 1966, the winter through to the summer of 1967, and from the beginning of 1968 until the autumn of 1969. Its migration across the week found the programme moved the first year to a Monday night at 10.00 p.m. Eastern time, retaining the time slot but shifting to Thursdays in the summer and then Fridays in 1967, on to 7.30 p.m. Wednesdays from the new year, and finally to Monday nights at the same hour in September 1968. The programming poses some fascinating questions: how many viewers watched ABC from *Batman* through *The Avengers* and on to *Gidget* in the first season? When *The Avengers* ended at 8.30 p.m. on Mondays during the Prague Spring, did people stay tuned to *Peyton Place*? And what did they make of it? For instance, when Robert Kennedy was murdered in 1968, ABC cancelled a scheduled *Avengers* episode, in the wake of accusations that television caused violence. Content analysts busily counted the quota of murders per minute in the series (Barnouw 415; Malone).

When Macnee and Rigg flew to New York in 1966 to promote the forthcoming series, he stressed the balance of textual trade and she her professional background, announcing that 'I've found the balance between Shakespeare and the sex and violence of the series.' The *Daily Worker* informed its readers that '[t]he two countries are exchanging precisely nothing'. Producers in both territories had long ago sacrificed 'credibility of plot' to 'ruthless, overplayed styling'. Other critics saw this as only a good sign. Britain's rapidly declining economy might be aided by TV as part of the Wilson government's export drive. It was even proposed that ITV licences be conditional on generating filmed drama that could be sold to the USA as per *The Avengers*. (Needless to say, this bold new *laissez-faire* doctrine of comparative advantage did not acknowledge that preferential Commonwealth purchasing facilitated profitable sales to places such as Canada.) (Gross; Rogers *ITV* 54; Macnee and Rigg, quoted in Lowry; Musel 'En' 20; S. Lane; Shulman; Purser, 27 March 1966; Black, 23 March 1966; Green 113; Rutherford 121).

Once the programme became a symbol of the 'Come to Britain' campaign its critical reception at home improved, at least until it became clear that Grade's Associated Television Corporation was selling concepts to the Americans before series were shot and then tailoring production to the terms of the deal. (Peter Graham Scott, who directed some episodes, recalls critics on the set saying: 'That guy's got his coat undone. No American goes around with his coat undone,' and insisting that 'lifts' become 'elevators'.) By the late 60s, the programme's main rival in the independent sector, *The Saint*, had left its origins in the stories of Leslie Charteris to replicate Peel-and Steed-style narratives. Prints of *The Avengers* were sold in non-English speaking countries with background sound intact but dialogue removed, other than in the Middle East, which plumped for subtitles. The transatlantic formula of high-quality vision, simple Manichaean divides, lots of action sequences, and definitive resolution polarised British critics between those who valued screen exports (like the *Economist* and the Prices and Incomes Board) and others more concerned about cultural specificity. Looking back three decades on, Macnee said the first Rigg season was the last consistent series, before the feeling of working for a US network pervaded production. Laurie Johnson says each episode was treated as a separate musical project, like films, rather than borrowing from stockpiled scores as is normal with TV series. Once the programme became popular in the US, transmission schedules required the shooting of episodes back-to-back; he was composing and arranging thirty-five minutes of music each week (Michael Richardson 10–11; Scott, quoted in 'Peter'; Mansfield 24; Tankel 84; Macnee 'Trente' 14; Mandell 29).

Macnee was hailed by critics for 'fine underplaying', a proper counterpoint to Steed's presumed wealth. American writers read him as 'a suave and sophisticated ministry agent who exudes Old World charm and courtesy'. (The actor's life is regularly contrasted with the role, notably since the publication of his autobiography, in which we are told of life with a mother glossed by the *Los Angeles Times* as 'a beautiful alcoholic who dumped his father to live with her lesbian lover, the formidable 'Uncle Evelyn', who wouldn't allow men in the house and insisted that Macnee wear kilts'.) Initial critical response to Rigg in the UK was mixed, veering between approval of the new look provided by shooting on film and an appreciation of her presence, to a wistfulness for Blackman's dry humour and some doubts about the 17-year age gap between the new protagonists. She became immensely popular over time. Macnee argued that: 'Diana alighted on us with genius and just took the show – which was a lighthearted comic strip at the time – and shook it and made it gossamer.' She too left, concluding in 1968 that 'discovering dead bodies and tracking Mr Bad wasn't very testing'. Abortive plans were then under way for another French-funded motion picture. A fortunate few have access to her obscure film portrayals of Emma in the dialogue-free Super-8 short *Diadem* and the serial filler *Minikillers*, a German production shot in Spain in which she finds herself on a beach surrounded by life-size Ken and Barbie dolls (Gianakos 527; Terrace 25; S. Williams; Lockwood; Purser 'Thoughtless'; Wiggin; Blyth; Furlong; Fakrikian 'Projets' 19; Koldys; Macnee and Rigg, quoted in Rosenthal 12).

Attempts were made to reuse the Peel *persona* in the United States. After leaving the series, she starred in a one-off drama, *The Assassination Bureau*, as a journalist whose karate helps her to defeat Telly Savalas. This was followed by the NBC special *Married Alive*, in which, as per her last *Avengers* story, a long-lost husband is restored. She also appeared in *Diana*, a short-lived 1973 NBC series palimpsest of *The Mary Tyler Moore Show* that substituted New York and the fashion industry for Minneapolis and TV journalism. Now she was making US $7500 per episode! This information comes in a *TV Guide* interview where she shares with us her passion for 'Shakespeare, always Shakespeare', while a reporter details the Rigg childhood in 'hell-hot India, where her father built railways' (Amory; Hano 32, 34; Knowles).

Ironically, some of the consistently highest British ratings were achieved for the final series, with Thorson as Tara King; but the money for its high production values was American, and the series suffered there by being scheduled against *Rowan and Martin's Laugh-In* (Tankel 88). *The Avengers* went into syndication straight-away, with a grand advertisement in *Variety* that called it 'efferves-

Childhood memories?

cent as champagne . . . sly as a furtive wink . . . hard as diamonds . . . and cool as a blue steel gun barrel'.

In 1975, Laurent Perrier hired Macnee and Thorson to re-create their roles for a TV commercial advertising champagne. Producer Rudolph Roffi proposed a remake of the series, which ultimately went ahead in 1976, with a second season following. *The New Avengers* exemplified the co-production deals characteristic of glob-alised TV drama since that time. Costing US $230,000 an episode, funds came from France and Canada. International sales were immediate. It screened on CBS on Friday evenings at 11.30 p.m. between September 1978 and March 1979, and was popular enough to be rerun and prompt another life for the original series. The same year, Quinn Martin Productions offered a pilot episode with Granville Van Dusen and Morgan Fairchild, written by Clemens, called *Escapade.* It was intended as a US *Avengers,* but no series ensued. After Lumley's later fame in the very different styles of *Sap-*

21

Alongside Jennifer Saunders, Joanna Lumley from her Absolutely Fabulous (BBC TV) incarnation

phire and Steel, Absolutely Fabulous and *Girl Friday*, this prehistory was explained to contemporary US audiences as her period playing 'the Farrah Fawcett of public-school boys'. But it nevertheless ranked poorly with many at the time, dismissed by some as 'Gallic rubbish' tainted with 'foreign' money and locations (Macnee and Cameron 267; 'Pre-Sales'; Terrace 26; Gabriel; Tarpey; Brooks and Marsh 58; Goldberg 296–7; Meyers 130).

Plans for motion pictures were announced periodically from 1980, via a CBS telemovie, an independent American production house, Universal Studios, Weintraub Entertainment (twice, once with Mel Gibson), then a *New, New Avengers* plan from Clemens. The old *Avengers* continued in syndication. In the early 1980s in Britain, Channel Four ran the colour Diana Rigg episodes on Sunday mornings, while Welsh viewers could watch HTV Wales reruns on Saturday evenings. ABC showed it at 3 a.m. Eastern time, Tuesday to Friday, in 1987. In 1990–1, A&E brought the Catherine Gale seasons to American television for the first time, as part of a 134-episode run that saw the programme stripped at 11 a.m. and 6 p.m. Eastern time on weekdays and then Monday to Friday at 10 a.m. and 3 p.m. and Saturday at 7 a.m. In 1996–7, Bravo cable ran it in Canada on Tuesdays at 9.30 p.m. Mountain time, and CBC's French network ran it on Saturdays at 3.30 p.m. while the USA saw it on Encore Mystery at 6.15 p.m. Central time. The series was also available on RCA's DSS satellite on weeknights via Channel 274 and TCI Encore Plex Fridays at 4.25 p.m. Sweden's ZTV scheduled it on Mondays at 8 p.m., and cable subscribers in New Zealand had a complete rerun stripped across Monday to Wednesday at 10.30 p.m. then on Sky Orange 7.30 p.m. Saturdays. In Wales, Channel FortyK and Sianel Pedwar Cymru screened the Emma Peel episodes at 6 p.m. on Tuesdays and 11.20 a.m. on Sundays. BBC 2 showed *The New Avengers* on Fridays around 6 p.m. and RTE in Southern Ireland showed it at 11.25 p.m. Wednesdays. France had dubbed Emma Peel episodes on Chaine M6 and Série Club on cable, plus English-language originals on FR3 and *The New Avengers* on TFI Video. Italian viewers could watch the original series in 1994 on CANALE 5, and it was also showing in Belgium on RTL-NI. Video cassettes were available from the early 90s. But in 1995, Lumiere, which has home video rights to the programme, withdrew all tapes from US circulation pending enforcement of its copyright against unauthorised versions. In Britain, it released all available episodes on a rolling basis from 1993. The Rigg and Thorson favourites came in boxed sets complete with introductions by the stars. The company called the series 'the jewel in our TV crown'. This time, Macnee had a deal guaranteeing him 2.5 per cent of the profits. In January 1997, it was reported that Lumiere had been taken over by the French company UGC, which was shutting down releases (Fakrikian 'Projets' 19–20; Cosgrove; Solomon; S. Williams; Dawe; Nichols; Brian; Dean; Kelly).

In 1995–6, the surviving principals from the original series could all be seen in their dotages. Blackman starred in the long-running sitcom *The Upper Hand*, the British equivalent of *Who's the Boss?* Thorson appeared in *Dr Atkins' Eat Yourself Thin* infomercials. As mentioned, Rigg presented imported British crime serials on US public television. Macnee was hosting a 'believe-it-or-not' programme on the Sci-Fi Channel, introducing a magic show in Florida, reading books on tape (Jack Higgins' *Sheba* and *Hell is Always Today* and Anna Pasternak's *Princes in Love*, with an option on the Bible), and narrating a documentary cycle about the Bond pictures. There continued to be talk of a film based on *The Avengers*, with Ralph Fiennes as Steed, Nicole Kidman as Peel, and Jeremiah Chechik directing. The *Daily Mail* announced in December 1996 that Kidman had dropped out and was to be replaced by Gwyneth Paltrow, with shooting planned for 1997. CNN's *Showbiz Today* reported that Julia Roberts had been offered the part that January, but then the rumours turned to Uma Thurman with Sean Connery playing a villain. This phantom film was its own saga. Meanwhile, fall 1996 saw CBS' *Mr and Mrs Smith*, a clear paean to the series, while spring 1997 brought *Spy Game* to ABC, a homage from Sam Raimi that began with a cameo by Macnee. (Marton; Davies; 'The Entertainers'; Dane).

2 *Pop*

This week, TV audiences will have a chance to see why Rigg's been called 'one of England's finest, most versatile dramatic actresses' – and perhaps, in the process, finally relegate *The Avengers* to its proper place on her résumé – when she joins none other than Laurence Olivier in a Mobil Showcase presentation of Shakespeare's *King Lear.*

. . . Impossible as it may now sound, the British press actually agonized, nearly 20 years ago, over whether even a refugee from the Royal Shakespeare Company like Rigg was up to replacing the popular actress who'd left the series—*TV Guide,* 1984 (Rosenthal 11–12).

'You English. Mini cars. Then miniskirts. You never know when to stop' – Russian spy, speaking from inside Steed's bowler after being shrunk by a machine—'Mission . . . Highly Improbable', 1967.

Diana Rigg, the new Judo-Judy, is all op art, kinky cat-suit and four-inch-above-the-knee skirts. Mod, modder, moddest—*Sun,* 1965 (Banks-Smith 'Cathy's').

Espionage has always been part of pop. The first *Sunday Times* colour supplement (1962) featured Mary Quant clothing, worn by Jean Shrimpton and photographed by David Bailey, a state-of-the-nation essay on Britain, and a James Bond short story. The inaugural *Observer* equivalent included fashions from France and stills from the forthcoming Bond move. Even *Tribune* beamed on Steed as 'a sort of innocent Bond figure'. The publicity biography summarised him as 'Eton-educated and Hollywood-trained'; modish dress meets conservative politics. Like pop, *The Avengers* and its signs demonstrate the impossibility of uncovering human nature:

Blackman with Edric Connor as Benham in 'The Gilded Cage'

forget moving beyond the imaginary into the symbolic, because you'll only reveal additional meaning anyhow in a depthless world. The search for truth in origins is asymptotic and endless, so let's make self-importance our sin and bizarre intertextuality our pleasure: the Pet Shop Boys do espionage. Viewers learn to derive pleasure from artifice, and the producers learn to make artefacts from pleasure: *The Avengers* was the first British programme to have a designated 'Exploitation Manager' who sold product placements to manufacturers keen to feature their latest furniture on the set (Booker 49, 238; Cullis; 'Profile'; Buxton 98; Mansfield 23–4). That was pop, wasn't it?

Hendry warned Macnee when he donned a bowler for the first time on camera to 'go easy on the high camp'. But for George Melly, the secret to the series was *precisely* 'pop camp', relying on exclusive knowledge about fashionable texts, clothes and manners that, oxymoronically, was conceived for and supplied to mass audiences. It represents 'the most consistently intelligent use of the pop camp tradition'. The violence is like dance, the sex implied, and the stories absurdist. In 1963, *Contrast* magazine says: '*The Avengers* is British television's first popular myth. As extravagant as an old Feuillade serial, shameless in its symbols and send-up eroticism, sharply contemporary in its attitudes, it gaily ridicules its own most sacred conventions' (Hendry, quoted in Macnee and Cameron 214; Melly *Revolt* 174; *Contrast*, quoted in Tankel 86).

In explaining this unseen phenomenon to its readers, the *New York Times* of 1963 describes the series as a domestication of pop that takes it away from teenagers. This makes the show akin to the world described in two contrasting American essays of 1964: Susan Sontag's famous 58 keywords on camp and Ayn Rand's defence of romanticism. Sontag refers to camp as a modern aesthetic sensibility. Built around artifice and privileging style over content, its fey and mannered human quality, often blurring the lines of gender and sexuality, is projected on to fashions and other highly coded material objects, using their complex signification to question perception and the possibility of perfect knowledge. Rand valorises *The Avengers* and similar thrillers for their basis in a conflict of values. This supposedly high romantic mode, founded in nature, establishes Manichaean divides between good and bad, with clear enunciative preferences for authentic heroism. Despised by the intellectuals, romanticism lives on via the taste of the public, 'flickering only in the field of popular art'. (The liner notes to *The Avengers* suite CD quote Rand extensively to establish the series' artistic credentials.) For the culturally neo-conservative yet libertarian gender politics of Camille Paglia, Rand's counterpart in our own times, *The Avengers* is part of the 'English epicene', along with Sir Frederick Ashton's Royal Ballet choreography, John Lennon's puns, Oscar Wilde's ethos and Lewis Carroll's romanticism; in short, image as an end in itself, derived from a complex interplay of formality and parody (Carthew; Sontag 275–92; Rand 132–4; O'Quinn; Paglia 550–1).

This approval from *belle-lettrisme* and the right is ironically in accord with some of the tropes of pop art more generally: both figurative and realist, it scorned the avant-garde separation of sign and referent in favour of working with 'the world', as Roy Lichtenstein put it. Pop's urban sensitivity drew upon everyday life and entertainment for its motifs. Britain's Independent Group of artists produced a manifesto of pop art in 1957 that reads like a printout for *The Avengers* (if always leavened by Steed's ability to breach the space of old and new, what my informant Niall of Perth thought of as a capacity to be 'in age and dress and manners the hallmark of the establishment, yet still so chic and always, ethically, on side with the counter-culture'). The characteristics include popular, transient, expendable, low in cost, mass-produced, young, witty, sexy, gimmicky, glamorous and big-business-like. *The Avengers*' 'flip coolness', its '[n]onchalance' mark the series out as part of that fold. For my informant John of London, the programme's opening titles 'were the 60s equivalent of *Elle* or *Vogue* – sex for the stylish'. They are also to do with self-transformation. 'Immortal Clay' sees Mrs Gale smoking her cigarette in a holder with a stylish confidence that naturalises the gesture, but it features another character intent on slimming and losing her Staffordshire accent in favour of a Home Counties sound. She is a generation behind Cathy in the behavioural coefficients of social mobility. The tone is indicated by script guidelines on Blackman's portrayal: 'sophisticated but *not* upper class'. So it was that Macnee found himself going to the theatre with Princess Margaret, posing with Twiggy, meeting Julie Christie and The Beatles, being photographed by Patrick Lichfield, and drinking with Francis Bacon – while foreign viewers were interpolating Diana Rigg into Lennon and McCartney's lyrics as the ideal figure of love. Of course there was a painful memory underpinning those old enough to recall not 'having it so good'. Interviewed in 1991, Macnee said: 'if you were cool in the late forties or early fifties – just after the war, obviously – to be cool really implied that you stayed alive . . . If you're not cool, you're dead. That is the basis of John

Steed's character' (S. Wilson 4–5, 37; Shulman; Rogers *Complete* 35; Macnee and Cameron 232, 247; Rivière 34; Macnee, quoted in Biederman 27).

Arthur Danto argues that pop drew attention to art history as a series of erasures, of canonical exclusion, rather than obedience to the immanent beauty of texts. By its very presence in galleries and museums, pop art made it apparent that the difference between commercial dross and aesthetic elevation lies in two areas: firstly, the power to tell history and control institutional space; and secondly, the power to theorise the democratic potential of everyday life and the liberating meaning it offers to artistic representations. In a similar way, cult TV co-opts or eludes aesthetic conventions that demonise the medium for its supposed failure to produce transcendence on the part of the viewer. High culture expects art to elevate us beyond the diurnal, beyond the limiting factors of body, time and place. Folk-life, by contrast, expects culture to settle us into a sedimented collectivity through the natural wellsprings of community, situating art *within* the diurnal, as an artefact of ordinary life. Pop idealises fun as the summit of cultural pleasure, suggesting that the other two discourses can be combined via a loss of self engendered by pop's paradoxically absolute everydayness. So *The Avengers Annual* can produce Steed as 'Bulldog Drummond with a beat, a hip Richard Hannay, a Wimsey who's with it'. Fun is the last imperial posture after Suez and the winds of change. Like chocolate, the programme is 'compulsive' *and* '[i]mpossible to take seriously'. Julian Critchley in the *Times* calls it 'camp as a row of tents, which is how we like it nowadays' (Danto 3–7; Frith 106–7; *Annual*, quoted in Chibnall; Blyth; Critchley).

Clemens said in retrospect:

> We admitted to only one class – and that was the upper.
> Because we were a fantasy, we have not shown policemen or
> coloured men. And you have not seen anything as common
> as blood. We have no social conscience at all. (Clemens, quoted
> in Fulton 24–5)

But this is a little imprecise. There was a touch of demographic inclusiveness in the early series. The distinguished Trinidadian actor, engineer and songwriter Edric Connor (Daggoo in the 1956 *Moby Dick*) made his role in 'The Gilded Cage' perhaps the most complex of Blackman and Macnee's enemies. And the camera lingers just too long on a still photograph of white and black children enjoying themselves together at a conjuring show in 'Death of a Great Dane' for this to be other than pointed. The series *is* partly about dragging Britain into a post-war transformation. In 'November Five', Steed and Mrs Gale encounter sceptical officialdom as they reveal a conspiracy: 'My dear chap, you're surely not suggesting this was a political assassination? That sort of thing doesn't happen in this country.' 'Dial a Deadly Number' finds Macnee and Rigg dealing with businessmen perturbed by full employment, high living standards and growing inflationary pressures. In 'The Gilded Cage', Mrs Gale enters a space-age, automated surveillance site, complete with voice-recognition device, where she works with gold bullion. Glistening edges, newness and a hint of the post-contemporary are on view. But the newness must always be tempered with an appreciation of the difficulties of modernity. 'Death at Bargain Prices' sees Steed and Emma confront a plot to destroy London driven by a 'father of British industry' who lives on the top level of his store in the Department of Discontinued Lines. Steed presents himself to Horatio Caine as an efficiency expert ready to improve the company's time-and-motion performance. Caine recollects a '[g]racious, leisurely, ordered time . . . when a machine was a thing of joy' and there was no obsolescence. He plans to 'turn their modern techniques against them' by blowing up the city with a bomb inside a new washing machine. But for Steed and Mrs Peel, the future must have a cultural touch as much as a technological one, to ensure that means-ends rationality is ironised (Mason 39). We shall examine these dilemmas in the chapter on the postmodern.

Clemens's quotation reminds us that TV drama is often exclusionary and unpleasant. But popular texts are read at specific spatial and temporal nodes by particular human subjects. Audiences of popular culture are relatively power*less* in relation to the means of production and representation, but relatively power*ful* as interpretative communities. This begs a question about the broader political significance of the productive economy and the interpretative one. The popular is marked by a division of conventional hierarchies of artistic value. European high art and the philosophical aesthetics of Western ruling classes are set against mass entertainment. Any attempt to transcend this high–low divide must deal with some definitional legacies. The first derives from neoclassical economics, in which unfettered expressions of the desire and capacity to pay for services stimulate the provision of entertainment and hence (when the product is publicly accepted) decide the meaning of the popular. This is a processual and quantitative measure, as opposed to directional and qualitative definitions that seek out originary, organic sites of the popular in the people themselves. Here is the conundrum: Do the mechanics of price confer value as an articulation of the rhythms of supply and demand, or does it arise as part of the guardianship of heritage, as a history that announces certain sites, texts and practices as indices of how we got to where and who we are? Is value economic or ethical?

Television in Western Europe has always had a tension between wishing to inform citizens and please consumers: the audience is routinely figured as a mindless creature that can either be educated or entertained. In histories of British broadcasting, this dynamic is sometimes used as a binary to divide the BBC from commercial services. But Reithian notions of uplift were always leavened by the lightest of entertainment, and commercial TV has had its component of investigative and class-conscious current affairs. At the same time, the BBC's early commitments to live drama and the classics marked it out from an independent television sector that was initially troubled by financial difficulties and sought to differentiate itself from the 'government' service. The discourse of quality television since that period continues to claim that, while people prefer on a case-by-case basis to be pandered to by commercialism, their overall sense is that they should be bettered by TV: hence the continuing support for tax-subsidised networks. In the USA, arguments for public television oppose 'the market-place' to 'values we hold dear, such as excellence, creativity, tolerance, generosity, responsibility, community, diversity, and intellectual achievement', a bifurcation between programmes that 'explained one part of society to another' and those focused on 'entertainment and relaxation', *The Avengers* is generally placed at the top of the latter (Schrøder 200; Twentieth Century Fund 4; Dunkley).

*Bertram Fortescue–
Winthrop-Smythe
(Jeremy Lloyd),
amateur astronomer
and professional
chimney sweep,
explains his class
background to Mrs
Peel in 'From Venus
with Love'*

British definitions of quality are inflected by the impact of sales to the USA under the rubric of *Masterpiece Theatre*, a commercial inspiration to costume history that is very hidebound in its aesthetic and social politics. Charlotte Brunsdon identifies four characteristics of such programming: sources in middlebrow literature, theatrically hyperbolic acting, costly production values, and a national identity dripping with the past. Lyn Thomas notes a 1980s addition to exportable Englishness: 'village greens and gardens, medieval lanes and churches, and wood-panelled interiors where log fires burn even in high summer'. That inevitably compromises an engagement with contemporary social conflicts, as local TV production is designed to attract overseas sales. Specifically, this means a projection into American imaginations about true Britishness. The landscape becomes literary, the class structure traditional, the city and the country heritage, and the industrial culture untouched. A purely historical engagement insists on freezing Britishness in a non-conflictual, racially unitary past. The careful work of US groups like 'Viewers for Quality Television', which circulates members' incomes to the networks in order to be thought of as a desirable demographic group, should not be underestimated (Brunsdon 85–6; L. Thomas 3; Murdock 171, 173; Lewis 5).

The Avengers has several of these qualities, but in a nicely contrary fashion that is blessedly free of any literary origins, other than a few situations drawn from Ian Fleming. 'From Venus with Love' plays with the British hierarchy: one of the bizarre group of amateur astronomers who form the local Venusian Society is Bertram Fortescue-Winthrop-Smythe. Much is made of his paradoxical life. Despite his name and dress – tails, top hat and carnation – he is one of a long line of chimney sweeps, drawing a bemused smile from Mrs Peel that brings out the strangeness of these juxtapositions. Publicity for the series repeated Macnee's stage and TV experience and his early life at Eton, alongside Rigg's formal training in Shakespearianisms. The age and style difference between Mrs Peel and Steed – either 20 years or 50, depending on whether you calculate it by age or demeanour – beautifully captures the heritage of modernity. As Macnee put it years later, the series found the two main figures jolted together across history: 'I was eighteenth century, but the woman was essentially twenty-first century.' In 'Castle De'ath', she goes undercover representing the Advisory Bureau on Refurbishing Castles and Stately Homes as Tourist Attractions; he is McSteed, a researcher keen to learn more about the thirteenth laird (Macnee, quoted in Hirshorn 16).

Unlike safely bland British costume drama that casts the viewer into a space far distant from contemporary citizenship, *The Avengers* staged a meeting of the past with the present. Perhaps this was an artificially comfortable encounter, but it did raise the question of how appropriate yesterday's Britain was for today's. The series' sudden shifts in diegesis may have required leaps of faith. But a very careful reading is called for in Nancy Banks-Smith's claim for the programmes as 'a true cartoon of their time' ('The Avengers'). Even the opposition between the new and the old is unstable. In 'Death of a Batman', Steed and Mrs Gale make fun of the young Mayfair crowd and reports in gossip magazines of its wild parties. They even mimic the accents of the smart set. This is no simple binary division between the woman as a sign of newness and the man as a sign of tradition; both are negotiating old and new ideas

*Delights of the
dungeon for
researcher Mrs Peel
and lost laird McSteed
in 'Castle De'ath'*

of British middle- and upper-class life. Later in the text, a member of the aristocracy defends himself to Steed by arguing he is 'a patriot, not a traitor' for embezzling funds to assist research and development by electronics firms. Steed rejects this account: means–ends rationality without proper procedure is wrong, even in the name of modernising the hierarchy to retain existing structures of power. At the same time, it is clear that conventional state workers are also targets. As Steed says in 'The Last of the Cybernauts . . . ??': 'Ministry types; no stamina.'

The nice point about pop is its combination of repetition and the new. Rigg's début, 'The Town of No Return', has a post-titles extreme close-up on a doorbell sign: 'Mrs Emma Peel'. Steed pokes the bell with his umbrella, very much the gentleman caller. Then a huge eye – referencing the logo of the Pinkerton Detective agency – blinks its eyelashes to welcome him. Our first sight of Emma is in black leather, fencing mask and foil, armed with the threat (or per-

haps the promise) of an alternative to the realist thriller. That sets the scene for off-beat entrances in other episodes. For 'Castle De'ath', traffic lights at an intersection read 'Mrs Peel' and 'We're Needed', signs from Steed that come from nowhere, a magic omniscience without explanation that is met by Emma's ironic smile. The same message comes as she is looking at chemical slides through a microscope in 'The See-Through Man'. For 'From Venus with Love', she is fencing with a canvas body marked by a spectacular red heart etched as the target. Steed enters, his umbrella skewering a calling-card that reads: 'Mrs Peel We're Needed'. She is decorating her apartment in 'The Hidden Tiger'. Everything is draped in canvas except red candlesticks and an open bottle of champagne. As another layer of wallpaper comes off, the words 'Mrs Peel' appear. Puzzled, she looks over her shoulder to find Steed standing before another wall, tearing off paper that reveals 'We're Needed'. In one episode, she lies around playing a tuba while

Diana Rigg epitomises cool

Emma prepares for 'The Danger Makers'...

giving a 'piquant exposition' (M. Williams 90 n).

How does this witty standardisation and predictability connect to notions of quality? The special skills used by different audiences to read such repeated moves may be more diverse, polysemous, and well rounded in terms of developing ethical technologies for dealing with the everyday than the predictable ways of reading social-realist one-off drama or historical mini-series. When Channel Four's reprise of the series began in the 1980s, the *Scotsman* brusquely dismissed the programme by contrast with Antonioni's *The Passenger* (1975) (Eveling). The comparison is telling: did anyone find it wanting when measured against *The Dukes of Hazzard*? Critical distance, beloved of traditional literary criticism, and ecstatic immersion, equally positive for cultural studies or cinéphilia, are both important. By using pop and tradition as female and male counterpoints brokered by irony, *The Avengers* pulls the two tendencies together.

There is an oddity here. The figure of tradition, Macnee, was in fact a journeyman. As he put it in 1993, 'I've done absolutely nothing significant since *The Avengers*. No quality whatsoever.' The repertoire includes roles in *Lobster Man from Mars* (1989) and Doctor Watson alongside Roger Moore and Christopher Lee as Sherlock Holmes. Rigg, diegetically the figure of pop modernity, was an altogether different figure. This paradoxical discourse about her has continued unabated over the succeeding three decades: the classical actress (Cordelia in *King Lear* or Cleopatra in Dryden's *All for Love* and *Medea*, for which she won a Tony Award on Broadway in 1994 while Macnee was appearing with Hulk Hogan in *Thunder in Paradise*) who plays down from her training by fighting evildoers dressed in leather rather than robes, and speaking with irony in place of rhyme. The two poles come together beautifully, along with their mid-Atlantic financial substructure, in the 1990s, when (as noted earlier) she presents the *Mystery* series on US public television. Draped in bizarre lamé outfits, and standing on a kitsch set that merges *Up Pompeii* with *The Importance of Being Earnest*, she explains in rounded, hyper-Anglo tones to corporate-sponsored quality-drama viewers about where Inspectors Morse or Tennison are in their investigations and how they got there. This suits the interests of the sponsor, Mobil, by elevating its cultural capital. Rigg represents a watershed between the values of popular and high culture: 'the kooky and the classic'. Interviews routincly find her referring to 'the legitimate stage', or other means of differentiating and valorising live performance and classical texts over the TV series that made her famous. She also argues that American actors are more emotive and gestural and less verbal than their English counterparts, a distinction between the visceral and the contemplative, the populist and the cultural (Macnee, quoted in Kelly; Murdock 177; Musel 'En' 20; Brown and Rigg 53, 55). No doubt this insight aided her performance in NBC's 1995 telemovie of Danielle Steel's *Zoya*.

Rigg was thought of at the time of *The Avengers* as a 'hippy mod', presumably slightly evolved from Macnee, 'the first of the mods'. (Defining Steed as a mod looks strange today, given the Edwardianisms of his costume; but he did wear ankle-high slip-ons.) *Photoplay* held Rigg up as the acme of innovation for its 1968 readers: 'In mod-mad London, where practically anything goes, the living room of Diana Rigg's helter-skelter pad is guaranteed to make even the most blasé visitor take pause.' The magazine proceeded to go over the layout of her 'pad' in great detail: an early life as Augustus John's studio, a huge bed with 'simple black and white Op spread' in the centre of the living room, and a mix of antiques with leather (Reynolds; de Blasio 35). Macnee provided a counterpoint – again, in character – on the topic of 'Swinging London':

> You can use Swinging in regard to the fact that it's damn near at the end of a noose. . . . This miniskirt boom, the peculiarities they're affecting . . . I met the most terrifying little girl. . . . She took me to a pub filled with drug addicts, homosexuals. Poor kids. (Macnee, quoted in de Blasio 70)

The point is not to evaluate Macnee on these positions as his own, but to see them as part of a field of knowledge inscribing *The Avengers* and its stars into particular positions *vis-à-vis* pop. They were placed in that field as people alongside their TV characters. In a 1989 interview, the venerable *Radio Times* wondered whether Rigg found it 'something of a curse to have the laughter of Mrs Peel, the archetypal 60s swinger from *The Avengers*, still echoing in her ears'. Her response comes from somewhere between the diva of *Medea* and the irony of the fatigued: 'I don't look on it as a curse. . . . Thank God one is remembered for something – and it wasn't absolute rubbish.'

But the truly interesting remark for archivists of the 60s juxtaposes the conditions of existence of TV production with its archival nostalgia effect. Rigg points to the variant forms of life that separated pop from politics:

> the 60s swung by me. I was getting up at 5.00 a.m. to go to film studios. I felt so out of it because the hippies despised people who worked. That wasn't the thing to do. You sailed through life doing something artistic like painting a T-shirt. (Rigg, quoted in Grant)

This is in keeping with Blackman's description of her part to Channel Four in 1993 as 'just an ordinary job'. Nevertheless, Rigg has also spoken of TV as her tutor in the 'economy of style', and clearly acknowledges an attachment to Emma in every sense of the word (Rigg, quoted in Musel 'En' 20; Rigg, cited in 'Entretien'). Gestural annotations of character on the screen require infinitely greater subtlety than the large space of the stage, just as time management is more akin to an industry than that sheltered workshop for high livers. Perhaps *The Avengers* was both, a place for us all to bask in moments such as Steed's quizzical exchange with the inventor of the cybernauts, Dr Armstrong. He asks: 'Is this your idea of progress? A cybernetic police state? Push-button bobbies? Automated martinis? Remote-controlled olives?' Pop has its way of opposing standardisation and a dehumanised industrial state that supposedly anti-production-line, quality television does not always provide.

... then walks the plank

3 *Fashion*

Rigg is too smart to fool herself into believing that *Lear* will finally stop people from thinking of black leather whenever her name is mentioned—*TV Guide*, 1984 (Rosenthal 12).

Who would have guessed that a gent voted one of the world's best-dressed men could have been raised by his mother and her lesbian lover to be a girl?—*New York Post*, 1988, on Patrick Macnee's autobiography (quoted in Macnee and Cameron, back cover).

Apicella décor, the high-camp detachment of grown-ups playing children's fantasy games, melodramatic production values, achieved by composing shots in glossy James Lobb toecaps and the chromium hubs of the less reliable GT cars, with handheld wobble for taut climaxes and camera teams lying supine the better to shoot up villains' nostrils.
I like it—the *Times*, 1976 (Coren).

Fashion is integral to all drama programming on television. Repeat characters need to be differentiated from irregular figures – and vice versa – and commodities are the way to do it. The mutton-chops and flared trousers of Rock Hudson in *Macmillan and Wife*, the shirts and jeans of Angela Lansbury gardening in *Murder She Wrote*, and the ever-present raincoat of Peter Falk in *Columbo* are defining qualities (Kaminsky with Mahan 64). But of course, the products that can be sold alongside the supposed sophistication of Robert Wagner in *Switch* or *Hart to Hart* are thought to be rather different from the alleged decency of Efrem Zimbalist Jr in *The FBI*.

The Avengers stands out because it needs none of the lurid boredom of Don Johnson, the twee domesticity of Stefanie Powers and Wagner, the 'her indoors' of *Minder*, the empiricism of Jack Webb's

Steed with his original partner Dr Keel (Ian Hendry) — a couple of spivs?

Steed with his original partner Dr Keel (Ian Hendry) — a couple of spivs?

Dragnet ('just the facts'). Ennui is out as style or response; irony is clothed and clothing for the series. (An early American version, *Honey West*, took fashion accessories as its keynote for the protagonist, played by Anne Francis: earrings that doubled as gas grenades, a garter/gas mask, immense sunglasses with two-way radio frames, a walkie-talkie in her compact, and a lipstick that transmitted radio messages. This redundancy gave the series a short life, its redeeming feature being Bruce, the pet ocelot.) In many ways, *The Avengers'* clothes and accessories *were* the gadgets that marked them out from US rivals. British critics like R. W. Cooper in the *Times* were wrong to claim that simple narrative quality lifted the series above *The Man* or *Girl from U.N.C.L.E.* Would you prefer Stefanie Powers' pill-box hat to Patrick Macnee's bowler, Robert Vaughn's cleft chin to Diana Rigg's pout?

At the beginning of the first season, Macnee and Hendry went about in somewhat tired raincoats. Macnee suggests they looked like 'a couple of dirty old men on the run . . . all cigarettes and dirty macs', moving between disreputable roll-your-own tobacco and an overly fey cigarette holder in 'The Frighteners'. Newman saw problems with Steed's clothing and encouraged Macnee to imitate himself more on screen. As Macnee puts it, 'that "self" had been shaped by eighteenth- and nineteenth-century influences'. The actor's clothing in private life matched the character's personality on screen better than the designated costume. Hence the arrival of bowler and umbrella. In preparation for the second season, additional refinements were made, including striking cuff-links and embroidered waistcoats, followed by cummerbunds and braided pinstripes. Voted among the 'Ten Best-dressed Men in the World' for 1963, he was invited to join Pierre Cardin and Hardy Amies in a new men's clothing line based on Steed's wardrobe. When his clothes became available through Bailey & Weatherill of London, young American men flocked to buy (Musel 'En' 21; Macnee, quoted in J. Wilson; Kelly; Macnee and Cameron 209, 213, 224, 231, 233; 'Dressed' 46).

The Edwardian referent is apt, if politically dubious. The post-Victorian era saw the emergence of the gentleman spy in English popular fiction. Duckworth Drew, John James Jacox, Ray Raymond, Hardcross Courage, Jack Jardine, Cuthbert Croom and Hugh Morrice made espionage an acceptable part of ruling-class amateurism, a sort of cricket at night-time that is conducted in sharp contrast to the miscegenate professionals who work for the Continental opposition. Unlike those lower orders, the Edwardian spy returns to his elegant rooms and decanters once the nation has been made safe (Stafford 490–1, 503). Steed's character is beautifully parodied on this score in 'The Charmers', where he and Mrs Gale are pitted against the Academy of Charm for Aspiring Young Gentlemen's Gentlemen. Ostensibly dedicated to teaching people how to hail cabs by 'thrusting' rather than merely 'waggling' their umbrellas, and the best way to pick up ladies' handkerchieves, the Academy is far more sinister behind the scenes. Operatives have concealed transmitters in their bowlers. Steed penetrates their front by posing as a fop in search of an Old Irascibles Fencing and Tottering Club tie. For Americans, Steed's umbrella (they often refer to it as his 'bumbershoot') was a defining and loveable characteristic of male Britishness (Andrae 117). Here, it was his entrée to outwit traitors.

Blackman's leather was directly attributed to Macnee, or more specifically to one of his old-Etonian friends who wore made-to-measure leather underwear and introduced him to an ex-army man who claimed the programme's ratings would grow if black leather and fetishism were introduced. When this happened, the leather became a major point of public discussion, encouraging the spread of the word 'kinky' into everyday parlance. (Macnee was, of course, aware that second skins can look most alluring given the right lighting.) Mrs Gale was known from the first for her clothes, designed by Michael Whittaker with a view to being six months ahead of women's fashions. Guns were kept at different moments in a garter under her culottes, in her armpit, and then in a compact. She wore knee-high boots, tailored leather suits and a trench coat at a time when such outfits were only seen in porn magazines and fetishist outlets. Her hat is a mannish quasi-bonnet in 'Immortal Clay'. For 'Death of a Great Dane', she moves easily between a very short-sleeved, skin-tight white T-shirt with mottled, cow-like markings, a pant suit for reclining on a lounge listening to South Asian music, and a sleeveless diamanté cocktail dress. This showiness follows the trend set in *Man of the World*, a series featuring numerous female guest stars whose wardrobes were exclusively created by the Fashion House Group of London. Fans of leather were, however, warned of Blackman's problems with her outfit: 'It creaks when I walk and smells terrible' (Macnee and Cameron 224, 231; Musel 'Violence' 14; Macnee, cited in Hirshorn 18; Macnee and Cameron 218–20; Black 'Undercover'; Keenan 73; Blackman, quoted in Musel 'Violence' 14).

'November Five' has a central camera set-up focused on her pulling on leather boots as she is told a nuclear bomb has gone missing. That formal juxtaposition of the diurnal (getting dressed) with the unusual (being filmed doing so for a thriller) matches the narrative shock of impending disaster. And it is not long before we see her throw a man over her shoulder while attired in leather coat and pants. That stylishness and competence match the décor of her apartment, with multiple mirrors, a tiger's skin for Macnee to lie on

All guns and garters for Mrs Gale

*Mrs Peel – minimalist
and modernist*

when visiting, and a bar. A remote TV signal tells her who is outside, she has a darkroom, and the furniture is minimalist and modern. Mrs Gale is draped over it in 'Death of a Batman' as a huge dog wanders past. Steed's home has a 'patent alarm system', foregrounded in 'The Charmers', and the requisite globe and telescope that establish him as sophisticated.

From the moment *The Avengers* was scheduled in the USA, fashion was paramount. The British producers wanted to maintain a contrast with Steed, but move away from leather in order to soften the image. Previews of the show detailed Steed's and Mrs Peel's clothing very carefully, noting Rigg's early career as a model. The *New York World-Telegram* called Rigg '[m]odishly dressed (leather outfits, boots, short, short skirts)' and Macnee 'ultra-Edwardian . . . suits with longer jackets, closer-fitted waistlines and velvet collars, embroidered waistcoats, curly-brimmed bowlers'. There was much debate over the materials Rigg actually had on, as word spread that plastic tights were displacing leather for late 1965. Three months before miniskirts appeared in British boutiques, one was purchased from Courrèges for her to wear on screen, forcing the *Sunday Times* to denounce the hemline as 'absurdly short'. The mini drew protests from the US networks and was soon displaced by the emmapeeler, a ribbed jersey or Crimplene jump suit with a silver-ringed zipper down the length of the front and circular holes at each hip. Her wardrobe was designed by Alan Hughes, John Bates at Jean Varon, and Jean Muir (for whom Lumley went to work as a model). Bates enunciated at this time his influential prescription for the female figure: 'narrow body, perfect square shoulders, long legs and small bust' (Macnee and Cameron 239; Musel 'En' 21; Lowry; Carrazé and Putheaud 185; Bates, quoted in Rouse 211). Like Rigg herself, this definition marks a shift from the fuller bodies of the previous era.

The Peel outfit is said to have been the first publicly available clothing collection designed for TV. Retail sales began following a show at the Courtaulds Fashion Theatre in August 1965 (Youlden 58; Rogers *Complete* 90). The initial Rigg episode introduces her target beret, which carries the motif of the 'Avengers Fashion Collection'. A press release compares her four-piece woollen separates to school uniforms, noting that the new fighting suits' stretch jersey

fabric offers greater freedom of movement than leather. 'The Bird Who Knew Too Much' puts Emma in a blue-purple-brown slip-like summer frock and a yellow A-line jersey dress. In 'Castle De'ath', her apparel draws an obvious contrast with a Scottish mansion and its owner. She arrives in her Lotus, wearing a tartan catsuit and a tweed oatmeal jacket. At a candlelit dinner, she contrasts with the men, who are dressed in lace and velvet, by entering with bare midriff, bra-top, modesty jacket, hipster trousers and ankle boots, all under the sign of lamé. She changes into a chiffon negligée and the fighting suit to explore a dungeon and torture chamber, topped off for the finale with a ciré panel. In 'The Master Minds', a wry English prep-school boy look is achieved via a jerkin and Beatle cap, while 'A Surfeit of H_2O' puts her in garters and a camel-hair coat. She is trussed up in black leather and horseriding attire in 'The Town of No Return', imprisoned on a saddle in stirrups. Resplendent in a bright-red jump suit for 'The Positive Negative Man', she is captured by a man with an electric thimble and tied to

a table. This becomes the opportunity for supremely confident Bond-style repartee. Confronted by a ghoulish figure in green make-up, Emma comments sardonically on his cosmetic sense: 'Oh, *spare* my blushes.'

Publicity stressed those moments when the Rigg/Peel personae merge. In 'The Hour That Never Was', it is said that her hipster-panted trouser suit, wide leather belt, sleeveless black top, and humbug-striped ankle boots are also worn in private, while her query to a photographer as to whether he 'preferred breasts or bottoms' is cited along with her feminist and Shakespearian tendencies (Wiggin; Auty; J. Wilson; Donaldson 'Transmission'; Rigg, quoted in D. Taylor 64). As one of my informants, Denise of Los Angeles, puts it, there is 'nothing flouncy or pink and bow-tied about her'. Sharp edges and angles to her clothing made Emma seem 'very efficient'. A fur-lined V-neck, as in 'Dial a Deadly Number', or a toga-style sheet for modelling work in 'Silent Dust', suggest a pleasure quotient, too. The delicious ambiguity of toughness, chic, perver-

Mrs Peel – restrained, as ever

Scolds Bridle used to Chastise the Nagging wife

Collar

sion and humour in her early black-leather outfits, the strongest memory of the series along with Steed's bowler, brolly and Bentley, are on display in 'Death at Bargain Prices'. Double zippers flow across the neck and armpits. Silver boots have a zipper all the way down the back. Everything is done up, everything is ready to be undone, and the body is tightly encased while the hair hangs free and flops across the face at opportune moments. For the second season, shot in colour, there are spectacular dress changes. 'Escape in Time' sees her in red evening gown for a hunt ball; emmapeeler pantsuit, black leather gloves, and a sky-blue coat; wide, short black jacket; an eighteenth-century lady's court gown complete with

beauty spot on the cheek; and a car mechanic's overalls. Suck on this, Madonna.

Miss King, overaccessorised

Hairdos were also important. When her hair is tied up and pinned back from the face, Mrs Gale stands for no nonsense; flicking back the strands from her face slowly reveals Mrs Peel's becoming half-smile; the creeping downward spiral of Steed's sideburns marks out the Tara season as dated; while Purdey's much-emulated pudding-bowl (a page's cut in 'The Gladiators') is a first for espionage heroines borrowing their look from schoolboys. Tara's introduction, 'The Forget-Me-Knot', finds her dressed like Irma la Douce on a bad day: tan shorts, elbow-length leather gloves, cheap-looking leopard-skin coat with fluffy collar, black belt pinched at the waist, black boots, and a shirt with a low-cut back. This is the ordinary person brought into the text. And Clemens may have

Steed as a model for 'The Bird Who Knew Too Much'

inaugurated post-feminism in *The New Avengers* with his remark that Purdey was 'so liberated she's been able to put her bra back on'. Others read her look as fashion-model movements and clothing that telegraphed a sylphlike fantasy world of gossamer, vaselined lenses and landscaped backdrops (Puckrik; Clemens, quoted in '£17m'; Clayton).

My informant Piers of Sydney says, 'I went through a bit of a mod phase because I wanted suits like Steed's Pierre Cardin originals. . . . I liked Emma's clothes as well, but that's another story.' Piers thought the outfits Macnee designed had overly wide and long collars, untapered cuffs, patch pockets, and a redundant second vent on the suits. Such is the discrimination shown by certain followers of the series! Of course, this was a crucial cross-over moment for Cardin. In the 1950s, his first boutiques for men in Paris evoked derisory, homophobic comment. But by the late 60s, Sydney's *Man* magazine advises its readers that Cardin, already known to 'your wife or girlfriend', is unleashing 'high-buttoning double-breasted suits', not to mention 'the cigarette-line trouser cut straight from the knee'. London's slightly bolder *Men Only* explains this new look is a 'masculinisation of the elegant image' that derives, *inter alia*, from 'the rectitudinous Avenger'. With the advent of colour television, British men are put on notice that they will all become 'peacocks'. The point is illustrated by a silhouette of a TV camera pointing at an unnamed figure with bowler and umbrella. Steed has become a sign of the future whose iconographic status transcends identification by name. As if to underscore the point about the new man, a sequence from 'The Bird Who Knew Too Much' finds him playing the part of a model in a fashion photographer's studio. The poses are quite fey and campy, carefully designed and directed as a counterpoint to the woman in shot. But he is foiling a counter-espionage plot, even as he stands there (F. Davis 35; Nelson 78; J. Taylor 'Dressing' 52 and 'Colour').

The actor's school years at Eton, with silk top hat, pinstriped trousers, waistcoat and paper collar provided a personal background to this stylised demeanour, modifying Newman's original idea of a George Sanders type. Macnee created the Steed image by borrowing from Lesley Howard as *The Scarlet Pimpernel* (1934), his father (a former officer) – and Ralph Richardson's Major Hammond character in *Q Planes* (1939; *Clouds Over Europe* in the USA). The Pimpernel was foppish but strong, hiding behind his feminised play a steely determination to preserve courtiers from the Terror. *Q Planes* had an equally compelling quasi-aristocrat whose flaccidity confused his adversaries with hat and brolly (he had an entire wardrobe of each item to choose from). Major Hammond 'hated' a drink, was surprisingly athletic, and offered a Steed-like self-description: 'I have an official status, but I don't carry a truncheon.' Macnee professed to have 'pinched almost all of Ralph Richardson's performance, down to the umbrella'. The sign is really removed from its referent here: Marcia Landy suggests the Hammond brolly was an ironic allusion to Neville Chamberlain. Following Oddjob in

The Scarlet Pimpernel — Merle Oberon and Lesley Howard

Goldfinger, Steed's bowler provides a direct Bondian reference by developing a steel rim (in *The New Avengers* 'Eagle's Nest' episode, it has a telescopic antenna for two-way radio communication). The umbrella also does service as a swordstick, gas-gun, and camera (in 'Escape in Time' and 'The Cybernauts') (Landy 129; Macnee and Cameron 64).

Steed is 'as conscious of a trouser crease as of an atomic secret'. He can be found wearing a kilt in 'Castle De'ath', dressed in pyjamas with sleeping hood and then as Sidney Carton in 'Too Many Christmas Trees', dashing about in monkey-skin for 'The Master of Minds', and adorned in stove-pipe hat, cravat and rural gentleman's suit in 'A Surfeit of H_2O'. The ABC press office issued a press release for the 'Christmas Trees' episode describing the 'His and Her mink

jackets' worn by Steed and Mrs Peel and her white-striped butter-scotch llama coat and guanaco hood. Macnee plays a double role as male model Gordon Webster in 'Man-Eater of Surrey Green'; Webster looks like Steed and is used by the Russians to infiltrate a defence conference (Macnee, quoted in Porter 41; Lockwood; Michael Richardson 7; Shulman; Donaldson 'They've'). Of course, as the 1970s beckon, what now look like kitsch clothes appear. Alongside Miss King in 'Thingumajig', Steed is offering us check trousers, skivvy and suede jacket, like someone puzzled about his position on American golfwear and the uniform of the Simon Park Orchestra who resolves the dilemma by leaning towards each possibility. After this point, it is no longer possible for Steed to say, as he had in 'The Cybernauts': 'It's that casual air of elegance – it always betrays me.' He is not alone, either. Nigel Robinson rather cruelly derides Tara's apartment as coming from 'the interior decorator's bad acid trip' (40).

The fashion consciousness of the series lives on. *Diana* on NBC

Ralph Richardson waves away in Q Planes

55

was promoted through the formal gowns Rigg wore, fashions for autumn 1973. *TV Guide*, which had run a four-page photo spread of the emmapeeler (available through Old England), called her new clothes 'the most glamorous in decades'. Consumers were invited to share in a US $995 two-piece halter-neck and waist-length jacket with feather trim, or perhaps an aubergine-coloured slip-gown with blouson bodice and dyed fox-shawl collar for US $475. Interested shoppers could write directly to the magazine for information on the whereabouts of these desirable items. There were other, less obviously commodified, references to *The Avengers*: a guest appearance by Macnee and two tropes in the form of a male relative in Latin America and a Great Dane to care for. In the final episode of the second *Absolutely Fabulous* series, Lumley borrows from her *Avengers* forebears, as well as her own current character's hyper-real transvestite-like femininity. Walking through Manhattan in an all-leather outfit, she draws admiring looks from similarly-dressed men, also passing for women. Thirty years after British and American critics either denounced the series as catering to 'leather freaks', or rejoiced in the 'guilty pleasure' that mixed 'the catsuited Mrs Peel' with 'Old-World Steed' in 'kinky situations', a certain clothing look continued to mark *The Avengers*, and vice versa. Lumley's new role sent up her former one as Purdey mercilessly, with a hypertrophied femininity displacing this earlier balletic mode, while Alison Lurie specified the Blackman gear as indexical of pornography and generating a public discourse of fetishism ('Diana'; Arras; Terrace 111–12; Meyers 127; Gabriel; Lurie 232).

In Alf Binet's classic definition from the late nineteenth century, fetishism describes sexual fascination with a particular object, frequently something worn by another person. According to clinical evidence, it is almost exclusively a male phenomenon, explained in one of three ways. Classical conditioning postulates a bizarre and exhilarating event, taking place early in life, that establishes a nexus between objects and pleasure. Research conducted during the era of the Peel episodes showed a link between fetishists and exposure to erotic slides that included pictures of women's boots. The second analytic grid is operant conditioning. Rather than focusing on a single watershed, this model depends on people seeking quite rationally to repeat earlier pleasures in masturbation fantasies. Finally,

the family is brought to bear via an association between fetishism and disciplinary child-rearing that suppresses sexual expression (Weinberg, Williams and Calhan 17–18).

Mrs Peel's colonial flower power

Fetishism is also financial. Wolfgang Haug identifies money as both a universal expression of value that allows comparison and measurement of objects and a mediating force that displaces consumption and production as barter with its pure signifying power. The price of a good or service (exchange value) takes over from the practical utility of what is being purchased (use value). A price then expresses the momentary monetary value of a need. That notion of built-in obsolescence and value bestowed via the market is a key to all commodities, popular or otherwise. They elicit desire by wooing consumers, glancing at them sexually and smelling and looking nice in ways that are borrowed from romantic love but then reverse that dependency: people learn about correct forms of romantic love *from* commodities (14, 17, 19). The contradictions embodied in this mutual embossing of controlled capital and ludic sexual style come out in the sequence from 'The Gilded Cage' where a queer-acting butler details each item of Steed's clothing: what it is, where it came from, and its price in guineas. This becomes the basis for assessing and reporting on his pedigree. And there is a wonderful doubling quality in 'Death of a Great Dane' to the relationship between Steed and Gregory, a gentleman's gentleman. The strange process whereby occupation and masculinity provisionally defray (while also embodying) the forces of class division is clearly on view. They bump into one another. Steed cries, 'Snap!' Each man has a bowler and umbrella, but Gregory knows to address his better as 'sir', for he is a butler. He is *dressed* like a gentleman, but he must also *dress* the real thing, and his demeanour makes the point; he estimates the cost of Steed's garments. When Gregory holds Steed captive later in the episode, he serves alcohol and smoked-salmon sandwiches. They have an understanding.

The term Haug coined, 'commodity aesthetics', concerns the division between what commodities promise by way of seduction and what they are actually about (35). It captures quite beautifully the way that *The Avengers*' stylishness calls viewers into its world, where the depthless perfection of hyper-modern or traditional clothing enables a surface ease that can casually ironise the most materially threatening moment. The only example from US TV that approaches this is *Miami Vice*. Its locations, clothing, sets, lighting and narratively unmotivated 360-degree camera action are luxurious to the point of seeming fraudulent to some critics: sign value has undermined the distinction between use and exchange value in a Baudrillardian world of weightlessness and excess predicated on the ephemera of fashion lustre. Style becomes a signifier of itself, of bright and flirtatious forms of life that take ornamentation as their lodestone, rather than any underpinning ethical or political rectitude (Rutsky 77–9).

The Avengers, by contrast, seeks to broker the modern and the traditional: crazy scientists and time-and-motion experts without a sense of proportion, along with the mindless landed aristocracy, are equally risible. Automation (the new Britain) and unearnt privilege (the old) are both flawed, principally because neither has a sense of humour. True modernity can be achieved in a stylistic embrace of

From male fashion icon to a follower of the Simon Park Orchestra

Spot the real thing: Blackman and Macnee at the 1963 Avengerwear Fashion Show

art and technology, where youthfulness and taste forge alliances via a surreal archiving of the past and consumption of the present. Vehicles are crucial devices in signifying this, as well as clothing. Steed's Bentley convertible and Mrs Peel's Lotus sports are guides to their characters. His vintage car offers perfect TV reception during 'A Touch of Brimstone', a sign of paradoxical modishness. Between them, the cars breach and express the space separating tradition from modernity. Press releases carefully marked changes in star transport (Thorson selecting a 'dainty and feminine vehicle'). The Lotus H-frame chassis with independent suspension was a true piece of British ingenuity, much admired by older viewers. For the younger ones, Dinky replicas of Emma's powder-blue model and Steed's green racer sufficed. My informant Michael, enduring early adolescence in Chicago and Pittsburgh in the late 60s, veered between cathecting on to Mrs Peel's body and Steed's car. Lotus told Clemens its association with Mrs Peel brought in US $5 million by positioning the car on the American market (Buxton 104–5; '"The Avengers" Change'; Clemens, quoted in McKay and Richardson 23).

This dual quality to fashion, where it is both an appeal to the supposedly natural world of sex and the contrived world of the commodity, is neatly troped in the 'Kinky Boots' single, recorded by Macnee and Blackman in 1963 and rereleased in 1983 and 1991. *New Musical Express* described it as 'perhaps the first Marxist novelty-number rap-record'. Elsewhere it was voted among the ten worst records ever. Kretzner and Lee's lyrics point to the role of the fashion industry and ancillary sectors in generating practices of consumption: 'Fashion magazines say "Wear 'em!"/ And you rush to obey like the women in the harem . . . Footwear manufacturers are gathering the fruits . . . KINKY BOOTS!!/Advertising men say "Try 'em"/And you all run amok to buy 'em.' A call to arms against the commodity fetish, clearly. At the same time, the series had its own political economy of modishness: while Mrs Peel was meant to be at the height of contemporary style, that contemporaneity had its own historicity. The producers designed her wardrobe to survive the inevitable lag between screenings in Britain and the USA. By 1967, programmes were being previewed for London TV critics at fashion shows, ICI and Povel in Germany issued *Avengers* clothes, and an umbrella was marketed by Knirps, with out-takes from the series as commercials. When combined with the release of thematic clothes and toys, this was too much for some, who saw it as a preference for mannerism over narrative plausibility. But years later, cult independent band the Television Personalities could think of nothing better for the cover of their first album than a photograph of Macnee and Twiggy at the Avengerpack fashion show of 1965. A picture of Macnee and Blackman at the 1963 Avengerwear fashion show, dressed in leather and evening wear, guns drawn, and mannequins strewn around the stage, still arrests the eye (Rose; Macnee and Cameron 232; Chibnall; Purser 15 January 1967; 'Dressed' 46; Rogers *Complete* 60, 277).

The referential qualities of *Avengers* style remain with us. Diana Rigg was sufficiently associated with the Lotus Élan for *Vanity Fair* to run a lengthy interview/test-drive report with her on the 1991 reintroduction of the line. When Bravo in Britain advertised a rerun of the series the same year, the emphasis was on fashion as much as narrative. By the early 1990s, vintage clothing boutiques specialising in 50s and 60s fashions were flourishing across the USA, with Emma Peel a recurring motif. As one noted Miami Beach celebrity, Tara Solomon, put it, she was 'the TV originator of the cat suit . . . she was ideally svelte and composed, and she always got her man'. In 1990, the *New York Times* said matter-of-factly that 'The cat suit usually conjures up a vision of Emma Peel, zipped into a stretchy second skin, sleuthing her way through *The Avengers*.' This was certainly true for clothes designers and journalists. Basco's 1991 scuba-style clothing was inspired by designer Ann Ogden's childhood infatuation with 'the sleekness and dash of Emma Peel'. Gianni Versace's autumn 1992 line of leather, which touched on sado-masochistic imagery, was associated with *fin-de-millénaire* despair. Walter Kendrich argued that it was part of the long, slow emergence of 'fringe sexual practice into the mainstream', the first signs of which had come with Mrs Peel. For the fall of 1996, Versace again borrowed an *Avengers*-style bodyhugging leather style for women. Bryan Lars's autumn 1993 'Super Women' theme was illustrated at the launch with slides of her in black leather, jump suits and boots, followed by models in similar attire. At Karl Lagerfeld's autumn 1994 Chanel show, 'superwomen on the runway charged out to *Avengers*-style music', while House of Krizia presented its spring 1995 Callaghan designs with reference to Peel. That season's International Home Furnishing Market for designers and store buyers was highlighted by Larry Laslo's stiletto dining chair. He called it 'my dominatrix look', a tribute to Rigg and other 'vinyl-clad vixens of the 1960s'. The rediscovery of synthetics in the mid-90s was announced in a welter of rhetoric about how hippy clothing values had held back the bold new future promised by *Star Trek* and *The Avengers* (Ginsburg; 'Dressed'; Solomon, quoted in Greenberg; La Ferla 'If'; Ogden, quoted in La Ferla 'Take'; Kendrick, quoted in Servin; Schiro 'Smiles'; Spindler 'Review'; Schiro 'Hollywood'; Laslo, quoted in Owens; Menkes 'Runways' and 'In the World'.)

In Britain, *Vogue* suggested that 1990s stretch fabrics made the futuristic look of the series more practical (Hamish Bowles, the magazine's 1996 European editor-at-large and a fixture on the International Best-Dressed Men List, is almost exclusively found in Steed-like attire). Designers such as Claude Montana, Katherine Hamnett, Lanvin, and Thierry Mugler all drew inspiration from the Peel style. The return of mod to Britain and the USA in 1995–6 was signalled to the New York market by reminiscences of the series as the first mainstream fusion of sex, fun and clothes. The *New Yorker* explained who Nico was to its 1996 readers by referring to Emma, and when *People* magazine ran a gossip-column item on the 1995 gala to benefit New York's Shakespeare Festival, it featured a full-colour photograph of Iggy Pop in an orange Day-glo suit that was described as a homage to Mrs Peel: Rigg and the Bard ironically reunited, exactly 30 years after the dross of TV had separated them ('Em'; Beale; 'Nico'; 'Startracks').

4 *Sex*

[Diana Rigg] always pretty much lived her life as she pleased: openly setting up housekeeping with another woman's husband when she was in her 20s; dismissing her own first spouse . . . as 'a kind of macho toy'—*TV Guide*, 1984 (Rosenthal 11).

In a comic-strip way, we kind of mirrored the start of feminism. We enabled a woman to get on to television and do things like toss men over her shoulder—Patrick Macnee, 1990 (quoted in Solomon).

'We're constantly kinky,' says an associate producer of Britain's *The Avengers*. 'If there's a choice between Emma Peel fighting in a wet dress or a dry one, we choose wet.' In swinging England, kinkiness is the label for any offbeat dress or behaviour, especially involving sex—*Newsweek*, 1966 ('Good-Chap Sexuality').

Most people I spoke to or corresponded with about *The Avengers* – dyke, straight, white, African-American, ancient, modern, in-between – articulated their view of the programme in terms of female characters, with Blackman, Rigg, Thorson or Lumley as their focus. This is hardly surprising when we examine the absence of women from the rest of TV at the time. Exhaustive content analysis of US network television from the 1950s to the 1970s shows, for instance, that women comprised only a fifth of characters represented in paid employment. Action series had especially strict segregation, with very few heterosocial partnerships. This was a 'male world concerned with the problems of crime' (Rhodes 23). Barbara Tuchman summarises the situation: 'Symbolically subservient, policewomen who have been knocked to the floor by a bad guy are pulled from the floor by a good guy; in both cases, women are on the floor in relationship to men' (531).

Apparent exceptions from the 1970s, such as *Charlie's Angels* or *Policewoman*, look passive and dependent alongside *The Avengers*, where Emma Peel 'was wittier and brighter than Steed'. There was some spill-over to other genres. Ethnographic research into fans of the *Batman* TV series found viewers connecting Julie Newmar's Catwoman to Mrs Peel. And Susan, Doctor Who's first female companion, was conceived from a weird dialectic between an *Avengers*-style woman and a screaming teenager. Leela, a later colleague of the Doctor's who was much more self-possessed, also worked with an opposition between physical abilities and intellection (Rhodes 24; Jenkins 37; Tulloch and Alvarado 210, 213). Just as *The Thin Man* saga stands out for its marital explorations alongside Hollywood's concentration on *forming* the couple, *The Avengers* is remarkable for its focus on the day-to-day wisecracking of man and woman. Sexual tension suffuses a relationship that is neither fully collegial nor straightforwardly amicable. They are not quite lovers and not quite co-workers.

If we look at the history of gender relations in espionage reportage and fiction, this becomes still more significant. Julie Wheelwright has traced a nostrum in popular accounts of spying by women as the 'poisoned honey'. Male officials, propagandists, journalists and historians have produced stereotypes of women seducing secrets from hapless men. Motivated by the desire for sexual and material power rather than patriotism, they are thought to prize the overthrow of men above the call of duty. The 'spy-courtesan represents the antithesis of the maternal bond', living child-free and ready to play on men's needs and insecurities. Alternatively (a favoured British anxiety during the First World War), she may infiltrate and pervert the domestic sphere. Beware the German governess, language teacher, and nanny carrying bombs in her trunk or listening at the door, as well as the cabaret performer or waitress preying on bearers of national security. Lloyd George was even forced to address the 'Petticoat Scandal' caused by German 'beauty specialists'. Mata Hari's name survived her execution in 1917 to become a recurrent myth in Britain and North America, beyond the Armistice and into the new Communist threat. The profession-

alisation of secret services shifted the position of women. By the late 1930s, they were popularly associated with technical as well as sexual expertise in espionage. The dancer and domestic servant were joined by the professional chemist (Wheelwright 293–7, 305).

Mrs Gale inspects

This amalgam served as raw material for *The Avengers*. Newman envisaged Mrs Gale as a cross between Margaret Bourke-White, the noted still photographer, Margaret Mead, ethnographer and theorist of sex, and Grace Kelly. Press handouts of the time describe Mrs Gale as a 'cool blonde, with a degree in anthropology, who married a farmer in Kenya and became adept with a gun during the Mau-Mau troubles'. Her husband dead, she aids Castro in Cuba until he embraces state socialism, when she finds work at the British Museum. In 'The Secrets Broker', she moves easily between lecturing at the London Institute of Anthropology and attending a wine-tasting, blending colonialism with the modern. 'The Gilded Cage' finds her explaining the finer points of the global trade in gold to Steed. Explaining her character to French readers 30 years after, the fan magazine *Génération Séries* called her 'féministe (un peu) avant

A frisson between Steed and Mrs Gale

l'heure . . . et vaguement lesbienne [a bit of a feminist before her time . . . and vaguely lesbian]'. It read off her sexuality from her black motorcycle and her coolness towards Steed. In 1990, *TV Guide* suggested Catherine Gale 'kicked open the doors for future TV heroines'. *Avengers* archivist Dave Rogers calls her 'a 1960s version of Shaw's emancipated young woman providing the conscience in combat with Steed's contemporary Chocolate Soldier'. Channel Four intercut Macnee and Blackman talking about their view of the programme's gender politics in 1993. She: 'Instead of standing by the kitchen sink . . .' He: 'with a bosom to take your breath away'

(Macnee and Cameron 221–2; Solomon; Rogers *Complete* 32; Winckler 10; Rogers *ITV* 54).

There was a *frisson* between Steed and Mrs Gale. In 'The Undertakers', he fantasises aloud about taking a trip together on an ocean liner. She blithely cleans a rifle, showing no interest in his suggestions. An array of guns on the wall of her apartment provides a backdrop to her reprimand of him in 'Death of a Great Dane': 'Must you be so callous?' she asks as they look over X-rays of a sick man; and she goes on to label him a 'cynic'. But this is to forget the treasured moment that finds them listening to music at her place. She is lying on a couch, wearing a serious lift-and-separate plus form-hugging clothes. Steed sits on the floor below her. Standing up, she lets a silken scarf fall on his head. He is enchanted. Macnee has written of Blackman's mixture of 'a magnificent bust' and 'lithe hips of a Boy Scout' (Macnee and Cameron 223): a phallic woman, in the sexiest sense.

Writers for the series worked with a set of gendered pointers on the two characters. Mrs Gale was straightforward and virtuous as well as sensual, Steed slightly untrustworthy, wilful, and exciting: a 'sophisticate but not lacking in virility'. Unlike Mrs Peel, Mrs Gale is a Monica Seles *avant la lettre*, squealing and screaming as she does battle with assailants in ways that made a few male viewers anxious. Blackman says she 'half-killed' some extras, and the pugnaciousness of her pose and face counteract any sense that the shrieks disarm her; rather, sexuality, power and the *look out* at the male form and its gaze are foregrounded. Her skills put her on the front cover of an issue of *Judo Illustrated*. In 'Death of a Batman', Mrs Gale goes under cover. Recognised as a spy, she tells Steed to get her away from the office. He says she must wait, offering 'Trust me?' in a two-shot. She asks, 'Why?' The effect is to ironise her dependency. At one point in 'Mandrake', Steed and Mrs Gale are watching slides of photographs she has taken of gravestones. He clicks his fingers when he wants to see a new image. 'Don't do that,' she says sharply, rebuking him for making her 'feel like a projectionist'. 'Death of a Great Dane' finds her explaining the technical specifications of photographic style to him while he makes sexist remarks about the wildlife birds she has filmed. In 'November Five', she smokes cigars with a politician, pointedly being the one to offer them to the man.

No wonder Blackman was hailed as Britain's 'new symbol of womanhood' (Rogers *Complete* 15; Teranko 88; Carlton).

For 'The Little Wonders' episode, ABC publicity made much of 'Cathy's First Kiss'. Press officer Marie Donaldson put it like this:

> Through thirty-three episodes and two seasons, the cool and immaculate Mrs Gale has remained inviolate against the advances of everyone from eligible business tycoons to the ever-hopeful John Steed.
>
> . . . But there it is: the leather is breached; the walls of Jericho have fallen, and on Saturday, 11 January 1964, The Avengers celebrate Leap Year—as usual, in reverse—when Steed, in the best tradition of his ancestors, plants a full-blooded kiss smack on the lips of his flaxen-haired amanuensis. Nothing like it has been seen on television since Marshal Dillon embraced Kitty. ('Little')

The *Daily Mail* captioned a close-up of the four lips with the headline 'First Kiss', but stressed that the embrace was 'in the line of their extraordinary duty'. She is pretending to be his lover as a means of penetrating a male-only environment. This subterfuge mirrored matters off screen: casting a woman in an adventure series in the first place, and then *not* having her romantically involved with the male lead, shocked network executives of the time, who continued to lobby for the pair to make it together (Gowers; Macnee and Cameron 222–4, 231).

As we have seen, sex was not sanitised out of the series, and the programme was hardly free from the prevailing modes of representing women: the video slick to a recent North American release is a colour studio shot of Macnee fully clothed and Blackman in bra and panties. Blackman has said she 'got quite hysterical' over policies that limited her character's conduct. And both Mrs Gale and Mrs Peel were frequently trapped by sadistic men who wanted to cause them grievous harm. (The need to balance shooting schedules with Macnee's deals for vacation time provided some of the stimulus to this focus on his partner (Alsop 16).) The set-up troped conventional horror-film methods of demeaning women, such as the evocation of panic and point-of-view shooting from the per-

spective of the assailant. The idea of disfigurement as a gendered
punishment, taking away woman's principal currency in a patriarchal cultural economy, is referenced in unknown men cutting up
pictures of Mrs Gale or Mrs Peel. That opening sequence is frequently followed by an invitation to an isolated country estate, psy-
chological torture, a sense of powerlessness, and then a turnaround
(see 'Don't Look Behind You' with Blackman, 'The House That Jack
Built', 'The Joker', 'Epic', and 'Murdersville' with Rigg). None the
less, as we shall see later, the women always prevail, sometimes with
assistance from Steed, in ways that show how resourceful and ratio-
nal they are. He provides a top-and-tail presence to mark equilibrium, but his partner is often the agent of change.

Blackman's previous 'English rose' roles in the cinema made for a
powerful contrast with her new character. The *Observer* dubbed her
'the leather fetishist's pin-up'. This assertive presence was instru-

Anxiety sets in

71

The long shot juxtaposes Mrs Peel's modernity (the clothes, the car) with rustic masculinity

Queanbeyan boy George Lazenby draws a disingenuous smile from Rigg in On Her Majesty's Secret Service (Danjaq, Eon Productions)

mental in her selection to play Pussy Galore in *Goldfinger*. Blackman's image from *The Avengers* shifted 'the Bond girl' from its Ursula Andress incarnation to a more self-possessed, powerful figure. For contemporary critics, her role as Cathy Gale touched on Bond's sadomasochism: Francis Hope described her as a 'Flemingesque prop'. (Rigg too went on to play the lead in a Bond film, *On Her Majesty's Secret Service* (1969), sharing George Lazenby with Lumley.) When Rigg replaced Blackman, press releases contrasted them like this: 'Emma is a younger and gayer girl and there is more warmth and humour in the partnership.' The person who wrote that publicity material, Marie Donaldson, was also responsible for the new character's name. Writing down the producers' requirements – that there should be 'Man Appeal' – she shortened this to 'M Appeal' and then spoke it out loud. This is my favourite creation myth (Maurice Richardson, 3 October 1965; Alsop 16; Yule 125; Donaldson 'Transmission').

The producers viewed Rigg as a British screwball star, a Kay-Kendallised Carole Lombard. The indeterminacy of her relationship to Steed – will they?/have they? – problematises its buddy format, with reversed styles of gender a selling-point. In 1965 Clemens said the producers made Steed 'fight like a woman' with an umbrella or honey jar to stage an opposition to Mrs Peel's martial artistry. 'The Town of No Return' offers a duel between them, with foils. Their sport finished, she informs him she has just completed an article for *Science Daily*. The episode concludes with Emma piloting them into the distance on a motor bike, Steed riding side-saddle. Rigg said, 'I never think of myself as sexy. I identify with the new woman in our society who is evolving. Emma is totally equal to Steed. The fighting is the most obvious quality.' But at other times, she claimed that 'Emma Peel isn't fully emancipated.' This confused some journalists. Robert Musel, who noted her 'boyish hips', concluded his write-up of their interview like this: 'A delightful girl, but I wish she hadn't felt it necessary to help me on with my coat' (Donaldson 'Transmission'; Clemens, quoted in Rutherford 576; Rigg, quoted in 'Good-Chap Sexuality'; Rigg, quoted in Musel 'En' 22; Musel 'She's' 16–17).

The programme's early policies on Steed's character stress sarcasm, irony, dispassionate ruthlessness, philandering and a flair for fashion. Later, he develops a well-mannered and self-possessed store of gentlemanly refinement, while Mrs Peel continues Mrs Gale's cleverness and problem-solving ability. Steed may be the commissioning agent who informs Emma about their assignments, but she is clearly the analytic half of the team; one has political and administrative knowledge and connections, the other has intellection and reason. In 'The Forget-Me-Knot', he asks: 'What's that - pology you're interested in?' 'Anthro', is her tolerant reply. There have been criticisms of Rigg and the other heroines to the effect that 'strength and capability are intertwined with an emphasis on conventional female beauty' or that realism has been sacrificed in favour of 'superwomen': the make-up never smudged, the men continued to admire. Such comments miss the variety of the female stars as well as the fantasy land of the story-line. Face, body, vehicle, clothing and apartment *must* be stylish if the diegesis is to cohere and the joke about the implausibility of it all be made. To repeat, the programme's gender politics clearly unsettled TV executives, and some programme buyers were chary of 'that lady' (Rigg), Kassaye Damena arguing that 'Ethiopian women don't throw people around like that.' The decision to replace Mrs Gale's judo with kung fu and tai chi was a softening of the role. The second US season was promoted to North American critics as an attempt to make Emma Peel 'more ladylike' by converting her form of fighting from 'karate' to 'gung fu'; sometimes this was said to be a form of 'feinting' or 'hoaxing' that deployed 'balletic Oriental dance movements' to confuse the opposition. When Rigg's US sitcom pilot screened in the 70s, *TV Guide* hailed her role as 'considerably more docile' than Emma Peel, noting that the plot called for her to hide the fact that she was taller than her prospective employer at a job interview (Curthoys and Docker 64; Gamman 10; Craig and Cadogan 221; Macnee and Cameron 239; Amory 'Review' 29 April; Damena, quoted in Green 297; Donaldson 'Transmission' and 'The Avenger' 13; Short 11).

As the series was about to commence in the USA, *Newsweek* had Rigg say of her character that 'the widow part shows that she knows what it's all about'. Publicity made much of 'A Touch of Brimstone', the Hellfire Club episode that was not shown in the States because of her 'sin queen' attire: a black whalebone corset, laced boots, whip

Each with their apparatus

and spiky dog collar. A 38-second sequence (why are these always timed when other segments commented on are not?) 'even offended the normally permissive British TV officials'. The programme clearly referenced subcultural codes from British porn of the 50s. Perhaps that was why it drew more viewers than any other episode screened there ('Good-Chap Sexuality'; Macpherson; Gambaccini and Taylor 32). 'The Danger Makers' has a telling scene in which Mrs Peel approaches Steed from behind. Their physical positioning conditions the dialogue that follows. She draws very close, neck to neck, asking him how to 'play it' with a person she must quiz. Steed turns to look at her, his face close to her breasts: 'Show him your bumps.' The alibi for this remark is that the character in question is

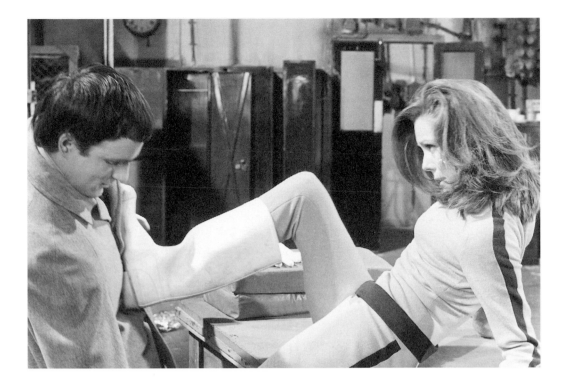

interested in phrenology. What reads as sexist is transformed by the banter in their delivery, her approach from his rear, and the set-up of the two-shots.

The sense of changing eras is beautifully captured during 'Escape in Time'. Apparently despatched via time travel back to the eighteenth century, Emma tells the villains, 'I'm thoroughly emancipated.' When the controls are reset to 1570, she is put in the stocks. A brutal man accuses her of being 'a heretic, a bawd, a witch – designed to drive a man to lust'. Her reply, from this somewhat undignified and powerless place, is to look up, toss back her hair, and offer the following: 'You should see me in four hundred years.' Back in the twentieth century, and the battle won, she looks at a woman she has just fought with, now in chains: 'Didn't we *get* the vote?' The stereotype of a woman tied down while evil men taunt her is also overdetermined in 'The Positive Negative Man' by a gaze back at her tormentors. Told she is dealing with 'a superman', Mrs Peel replies: 'His pectorals are *far* from perfect.' Frustrated, they counter that 100 such men, generated from the force of electricity,

'The Positive-Negative Man' Howarth (Michael Latimer) feels the force of Mrs Peel's boots

will destroy the government and take over society. 'What if there's a power cut?' is her riposte. 'The Cybernauts' episode sees Emma researching the holdings of murdered industrialists in the import–export, automation and electrical businesses. When Steed describes the victims as 'all in the top bracket', she adds 'where the vultures gather'. This scepticism about the patriarchal domain of capital is shown to be very apposite as the story develops. Mrs Peel directly encounters sexism at a karate school where the chief instructor says, 'It is difficult for a woman to compete in such company.' Her counter is good-humoured but with an edge: 'It's the idea of competition that appeals to me.' She defeats an opponent and makes her point. The ironic deployment of strong female sexuality in concert with physical force is exemplified in 'The Gravediggers'. Mrs Peel is on the ground. Steed, standing, holds a villain between her legs. She closes them around the man's head, scissoring him into a nearby pond.

After Thorson was selected to replace Rigg, the discourse on her tells us where the producers saw the programme going. Publicists suggested she was chosen because she looked like Shirley MacLaine,

Tara and her Lotus Europa

was five feet nine inches tall, 'and 38 inches elsewhere'. Clemens described her as 'sexier, more pneumatic in build, with a bosom and hips'; anxiety about her 'thrusting femininity' was modified by the belief that she was 'completely mouldable'. Because the producers believed that a 'Harlow look' was in vogue, they dyed her hair blonde. It broke off, leaving a sizeable bald spot. The decision to revert to her natural colour then necessitated the wearing of a wig. Thorson was said to want a decidedly sexual relationship between her character and Macnee's, and was quoted as favouring topless bathing, not wearing brassières, and seeing her role as using 'sex appeal rather than force' to get what she wanted from men. (Clemens wanted the character to express more fear than had been the case with the previous stars.) To critics like Banks-Smith, swinging a handbag rather than fighting made her 'a far more probable woman' than her predecessors. And in their scopophilic modes, my informants Tony of Wigan and Graeme of Sydney deemed her the most exciting of the female leads. Thorson was forever reshooting fight scenes where a combination of action and a miniskirt revealed underwear too dire for US network executives (they somehow didn't object to her code name of Agent 69). My informant Ann of Indiana was mortified by these changes: 'She literally hit people with her pocket book' (Clemens, quoted in Musel 'Can'; Banks-Smith 26 September 1968; Robinson 40; Fiddy 'Dog').

The New Avengers made a very public and lengthy search for a leading woman. Joan Bakewell likened the eventual choice, Lumley as Purdey, to 'a hockey captain attending a royal garden party' (but then Milton Shulman had summarised Rigg as having a 'hockey captain's walk' a decade earlier). Richard Afton went far enough to remark that 'sex has taken a long holiday', and Lumley looked back on it from the queer/libertarian-feminist credibility of *Absolutely Fabulous* to describe her Purdey as 'a huge disappointment, sexwise' (Bakewell 723; Afton 'Boring' and 'It's a Load'; Lumley, quoted in Puckrik). In 'The Last of the Cybernauts . . . ??', she and Gambit are discussing the history of cybernauts. Purdey: 'I didn't mention Mrs Emma Peel.' Gambit: 'You never do. Tut, tut, tut. I'd been meaning to ask you about that.' Emma is too close a rival to be spoken of, yet too inevitable an audience memory to be ignored. Purdey's makeover sequences in 'Faces' offer a nice set of transformations, however. At one moment she is a Salvation Army officer in sensible shoes visiting a hostel for homeless men. Then she is 'Lolita', complete with permed wig, long pearls, Cockney voice, a wiggle in her walk, comprehensive eye-shadow, and a nice line in 70s lip-gloss. This is the Lumley that made *Absolutely Fabulous* its own camp form.

And while Purdey's chiffon and silk softened her by contrast with women from the previous series, she was described in publicity by Ray Austin, stuntman turned director, as 'the most complete sexual animal'. An unnamed production team member found her black stockings and suspenders 'dead kinky'. The *Sunday Mirror*'s TV critic concurred: 'luscious Lumley is a turn-on', while Clive James could be relied upon to refer to her 'amazing pair of legs which go all the way up to her mouth, which in turn goes all the way across to each ear'. It was reported that a press screening found Kingsley Amis lashing out wildly with his feet each time Purdey executed a kick. The final Cybernauts story has the ghastly Felix Cain striking at a blown-up cut-out photograph of Purdey, his prosthetic hand scything through the space between her legs. Then we cut to a shot with a view of her from behind as she is bent over practising ballet. The conventional male gaze of horror film has been engaged. By the time of Bravo's mid-90s reprise, she had passed into a lost golden era of sexy women, enchanting new generations of nostalgic male critics. At these times, we have to say that sections of British journalism and screenwriting should go over their feminist film theory one more time. Meanwhile, Macnee was publishing a promotional memoir in *TV Times* magazine in which he said that he believed Steed had slept with all his partners (Short 10; James; Banks-Smith 'The Avengers'; D. Thomas; Peter Forster).

What of *The New Avengers*' unwieldy third object, Gambit? Hunt summed up his character's relationship with Purdey as 'based on a promise: *one day it will happen*'. Some might see him as the necessary triangulation of mimetic desire (like Tara's German boy in 'They Keep Killing Steed'): the relationship between the men attains its shape via interaction with her. But he was popularly regarded as spoiling and deflecting the sexual tension and ambiguity between Steed and the women, a paradoxically emasculated subject, prone to 'preening himself like a randy hairdresser looking for trouble on Brighton promenade' (Hunt, quoted in Short 11; Coren; Murray; Dunn). In 'The Eagle's Nest', the two men talk on the telephone. Steed says 'I want Purdey,' in a tone of professional urgency. Gambit's riposte of 'Who doesn't?' is the first reference to her in the new series. It tells us more than we need to know. The boys' clubby silences in 'K is for Kill' frustrate Purdey so much that she cries out, Wittgensteinian that she is, like a dental sufferer: 'I'm a girl, I'm a girl.' They turn. 'I'm a girl, and I'll not let that fact go unnoticed.' 'Target' finds the men eliding their speech, merging thoughts while Purdey listens. She differentiates between them for Gambit's benefit in 'Sleeper' by remarking of Steed that he, unlike the younger man, 'doesn't need a little black book'. After Gambit has woken Purdey by tossing her out of bed, she lies on the floor, impeccably made-up, while soft, saccharine music plays. When they meet up, Steed asks about her 'special knowledge' of a missing agent: 'Didn't you and he . . . uh?' 'Certainly not,' she replies, 'George is a gentleman.' Smirking, Steed says: 'That's no criterion. If it were, all of us gentlemen would be extinct.' Later she tries to climb through the window of his hotel room. Steed complains: 'You can't do that. Gentleman's bedroom? Very, very dangerous.' Purdey says the unsayable: 'But you're no gentleman.' Steed: 'That's where the danger lies.' In one sense, this represents a return to the somewhat salacious and caddish Steed of the Gale era, even though his status as an elder appears to remove him from sexual competition.

In effect, Gambit was the viewer brought into the action: the younger man in thrall to Steed and taken with Purdey, he is that most mundane of viewers, the straight white male, finding himself part of the diegesis without any element of fantasy in his character (the *Evening News* called him 'bovine'). If Tara is the everyday female spectator who is given a part, Gambit is her male equivalent. Steed is even forced to reproach him in 'Faces' for using a pump-action shotgun while clay-pigeon shooting: 'not a gentleman's gun'. But he's not really annoyed with Gambit: 'you can't help your background'. Such folk do not belong in *The Avengers*. We should be left to watch, like Macnee's role in the reprise, 'indulging the young relatives by taking part in sophisticated, melodramatic outdoor charades at a country house weekend' (Afton 'Schoolboy'; Usher).

But then no. Men are for the taking. The way they look, smell,

Steed's Bentley   hold themselves and treat others are up for audit. Recent analyses of the North American labour market, for example, suggest that wage discrimination by beauty is as prevalent among men as women. They are subject to the power of looking as never before. Consider some recent shifts in the discourse of advertising. From May 1967, Sélimaille ('Ceinture noire') promoted itself through sharply focused close-up nude male photographs, and English teenage boys of the early 1970s were encouraged to buy underpants by being told that 'Mother wouldn't like it'; these items would 'awaken the beast in you'. This was the era of Andy Warhol's cover for the Rolling Stones' *Sticky Fingers* (1971). It showed form-fitting jeans from belt to upper thigh, with the penis in hyper-outline, and a zipper to emphasise the central point at issue (Hamermesh and Biddle; Haug 168 n. 61, 84, 86).

Macnee was not immune to these trends. Despatched to nutritionists and health farms to lose weight for his role as Steed, he was put on a strict diet of 'lentils, crushed oyster shells and prune juice', shedding 28 pounds in one 1968 fast. He and Thorson were prescribed an amphetamine, Durophet, to lose weight. And there was certainly great ambiguity in his portrayal of masculinity. In the earlier series, the homosociality between Hendry and Macnee is very striking. In 'The Charmers', they seem intimate, almost loving, with Macnee sexy and Hendry gruff. There is just the right pointedness in the performances. Clemens suggests, 'we could never have made *The Avengers* in America. They would never have allowed us to have an effete-looking hero in a bowler hat carrying an umbrella' (Macnee and Cameron 214, 251; 'An Edwardian' 20; Clemens, quoted in Sutcliffe 30). The web site dedicated to *The New Avengers* describes him as: 'the perfect English gentleman, yet always working with the most liberated of female colleagues without discrimination or dissent'. Others enjoy mocking this persona, but perhaps they have a secret admiration for its bizarre blend of phlegmatic wit and controlled parody. This is in keeping with what the producers and publicists kept announcing they were doing. Consider a press release on Steed's early life, from 1962:

> well-to-do, with an Old Etonian background, a sophisticated taste in living, a flair for clothes, an eye for a comely wench and a not too fastidious ruthlessness in getting his own way. A Regency buck, in fact, twentieth-century style. (Quoted in Black 'Undercover')

Well, yes, but then again, maybe not: such a figure reads like an obnoxious buffoon and sleazy user. In 'Dial a Deadly Number', he has the following exchange with a young woman:

> *She:* You're tactful.
> *He:* Not tactful, optimistic. And I admire a woman with a past.
> *She:* What's optimistic about that?
> *He:* The hope that history may repeat itself.

As my informant Colin learnt from Clemens, there was a Harry Flashman influence somewhere in this mix. While Macnee certainly had a touch of the spiv in the early portrayals, by the time the dandy element was there his manner was subtle and above all light of touch, quick to self-parody (in fact, embodying it as a perfor-

mance style: the pat of the hat, the twirl of the umbrella). The gentlemanly character represented a complex negotiation of varying
masculine codes, or forms of life: undercover urban grit and
exploitation, old-world charm in a knowing contemporary context,
and a glint in the eye that loves to endure masochistic flirtation and
denial with female leads. In an early Rigg episode, 'Death at Bargain
Prices', we can see some cross-over between an old and new Steed.
Mrs Peel is working in the ladies' underwear section of a department store. He leers at the bare breasts of a mannequin she is dressing while referring to Emma being taken to the 'bosom' of the
company. She gives him what we might call a look and lets him
know he 'should fit in rather well' at the Department of Discontinued Lines. Later in the programme, he visits her apartment in
search of sympathy and tenderness following an attack. She is too
preoccupied writing a paper on thermodynamics to care for his
wounds. Seeking a point of contact, he tries the C.P. Snow line, juxtaposing the sciences with the humanities, an alibi to stay the night
as a means of breaking this regrettable divide between the two cultures. She sends him on his way.

In 'Mission . . . Highly Improbable', Steed is reduced in size to a
miniature figure. We cut to an extreme close-up of Mrs Peel. Eyebrows raised, she says: 'Tell me, Steed: is *every*thing to scale?', later
pondering 'I'm not sure I shouldn't keep you like this. It's one way
to bag a man.' When he is enlarged again (and the context for this
dialogue is the conclusion to a perilous encounter) the following
happens:

> *Peel:* Well?
> *Steed:* Back to normal.
> *Peel:* Everything?
> *Steed (turning three hundred and sixty degrees):* Everything.

Everyone knows what they are talking about, that Steed would want
to guarantee his sexual equipment to the discerning partner. While
producer Julian Wintle avowed '[t]hey're not sleeping together',
Rigg suggested the picture was less clear in her mind. 'Escape in
Time' includes two passionate clinches as Steed and Mrs Peel are
tailing a suspect; but the mode of doing so is itself hypertrophied,

The male gaze evoked in 'Death at Bargain Prices'

Reduced in size for 'Mission... Highly Improbable', Steed shows his mastery of rotary dialing

coming as it does in a very stagey, back-lot sequence where people buy large children's animal toys from a shop as passports to a criminal network. Still, Peel and Steed had *something*, as she said: 'My physical relations with him are, to put it mildly, ambiguous. They're certainly not active on the screen. They might have been in the past or then again they might be in the future' (Rigg, quoted in Musel 'En' 22). There are further resonances here with Ralph Richardson's Major Hammond of *Q Planes*, who refers to his sister as 'darling' and has an unconsummated flirtation with a society woman that is stalled by his continual inability to talk to her other than on the telephone because of his spy work.

A tense triangulated desire emerges, beyond even the structural arrangement of *The New Avengers*, when Steed encounters rivals for Emma's attention: the Honourable John Cartney from 'A Touch of Brimstone' or Paul Beresford in 'Return of the Cybernauts'. She describes Cartney to Steed as 'handsome and dynamic; very compelling . . . quite fascinating'. The visual composition presents a beautiful counterpoint to this appreciation of another man. Steed and Mrs Peel are in a close-up two-shot. She is a quarter turned towards him and he is in profile. 'And while you were agog with one another,' he says irritatedly. The jealous response draws her in. She leans towards his face, contradicting her distancing words. He is equally annoyed by Beresford:

> *Steed:* You like Beresford, don't you?
> *Emma:* There's nothing to dislike about him, is there?
> *Steed:* No, but I'm sure I'll find something.

When Beresford calls her 'delectable', Steed is again cross. She counters with '[y]ou're quite pretty yourself' before reprimanding him: 'Steed, you're jealous.' 'Just thoughtful,' he replies.

Jealousy is available to both parties. A hyper-ambitious, Tayloristic bureaucrat in 'The Positive Negative Man' flirts with Steed via jibes delivered over correct civil service procedure. Her orthodox regimentation and passion for secrecy contrast with his unusual style. She keeps keys to a filing cabinet in her garter belt, however; a clue to another side. As this terpsichory is played out, Mrs Peel leaves the room, reminding Steed archly to return the key. He meets

the bureaucrat again fly-fishing in a stream. She says only red-card holders are granted access to top-secret material. He removes his bowler to reveal a red card. In a later scene, Emma kicks Steed to quieten him and deliberately trips over someone, offering 'I don't usually fall for strangers' as she does so. We then cut to Steed interrogating her:

The oleaginous Paul Beresford (Peter Cushing) from 'Return of the Cybernauts'

> *Steed:* . . . to plumb the depths of utter banality with 'I don't usually fall for strangers.'
> *Mrs Peel:* It was a corny situation, calling for corny measures.
> *Steed:* And the kick on the shins?
> *Mrs Peel:* Oh, that? I just felt like that.

She speeds off, leaving him behind.

In the USA, much play was made of Macnee's sprawling, contradictory biographical legend, oscillating between 'the staid, stylish, slightly stuffy' Steed and 'a tanned West Coast beach bum' actor, at

Sean Connery and Honor Blackman in Goldfinger *(Danjaq, Eon Productions)*

times reportedly related by family ties to any and all of David Niven, Robin Hood, Robert the Bruce, Charles II, and Mary, Queen of Scots. In 1968, *TV Guide* sought the truth of the man. It went boldly into his London flat, noting with approval the 'concealed' hi-fi system, but registering distress at the one 'jarring note' (a television set) and confusion at his clothes, which mixed an Edwardian suit with 'hippie beads'. Macnee himself was open about the 'years of lashings' suffered from secondary education's 'swish of that vicious rod' and its role in his personal formation, juxtaposing public school with his life on a Californian nudist colony (Macnee and Cameron 65, 298 n., 258; Musel 'En' 21; 'An Edwardian' 18).

Mrs Gale sardonically refers to Steed as 'a man-about-town'. Here is our key: whether spiv or fop, Steed is destabilised by his partner. The advertising executive smart man of the 60s is outclassed and made to know it. Mrs Gale and Mrs Peel are both formed via life overseas in the outposts of empire. They look back at Britain in full working knowledge of its definition against and among its colonial territories, and even have academic qualifications on the topic. This made them narrative figures of historical power to match their clothing ensemble. As the *Daily Mail*'s reviewer Peter Black said of Blackman in 1962, 'What a horrible discomforture awaits any crook who tries to reach the woman in her.' She continued on her way as a feisty representative of the desiring yet autonomous woman, evidenced in her famous remark about acting with Sean Connery: 'I think he's got a pair of the best eyes that have ever been seen on screen, apart from anything else he might have – and there's plenty of *that*' (Black 'Undercover'; Blackman, quoted in Yule 127).

When Channel Four reran the Blackman years in the 1990s, it prefaced the screenings with a dialogue between the stars (Steyn). Macnee emulated the doublesidedness of his character and *the* conceit of the series: 'If you're working with a woman every day you don't sexualise with her. [Pause] I'm joking, of course.' Then again: 'You don't call someone Mrs Gale whom you've been to bed with.' There's a wonderful moment in 'The Town of No Return' when Steed and Emma are staying in a village pub. He leaves her room late at night, announcing that his cat-like tread will permit a discreet search of the premises. She listens by the door, a dubious look on her face as he moves around the building. He returns and is interrogated: 'What happened to pussy-footed pussy?', responding in turn with 'Isn't it time you were in bed?' A bottle of liqueur held in his hands barely separates them. Fade out. In 'The Forget-Me-Knot', they both lose their memories. She believes herself to be Steed and he confuses her with Miss King. They re-establish identities:

> *Mrs Peel:* Talking of forgetting; just to remind me, are you the man who [smiles]?
> *Steed:* I'm afraid so.

John le Carré calls spying 'the passion of my time' (270). And there *is* something truly passionate about this least typical of bureaucratic pursuits. Years later, Rigg looked back on the era like this: 'kinky. I always seemed to be strapped into a dentist's chair with my feet in the air,' and Macnee tried to scotch rumours that his early childhood spankings at prep school and Eton had left him with a lifelong taste for sado-masochistic sex (Rigg, quoted in 'Crib'; Kelly). But there is that wonderfully ambiguous moment in 'Death of a Batman' when Steed removes Mrs Gale's boots by standing with his back to her, the boots held between his legs as he pulls, hard and pleasurably.

Some things fade, but others remain. The on-line *Wetzine*, dedicated to 'the perv world', has run a description of *Avengers* episodes because 'take a cross section of British perverts in between the ages of thirty and fifty, and you will find that most will rate *The Avengers* as having something to do with it!', while Biba Leathers' 1990s advertisements for jumpsuits featured a woman with a Purdey cut but Peel attire and gun ('Biba').

During the course of my research for this project, I spent some moments in a Charing Cross phone box, in the way that rigorous fieldwork often requires. As I waited for my call to go through, I picked up a card left there advertising the opportunity to '*Turn your* TV Fantasy *into* Reality' by calling a Mayfair number. This message was bracketed by images of a man and a woman. The male figure was clearly Steed-like: the bowler, carnation and suit were present, and even the slightly quizzical stoop. I went back to where I was staying to process this excellent finding with friends. True validation of my *Avengers* study was assured, along with major sales. Perhaps I could even do a deal with the people in Mayfair to send out copies of the book as part of their service. Then my hosts pointed out that 'TV' stands for more than 'television' . . . . Kinky, those English.

5 *Genre*

The bosses back home were like Little Bo Peeps compared to the money men of the USA. Seated in a boardroom before a pack of fat cats, I longed to vanish underneath the plush carpet. Then a stentorian voice boomed, 'Okay, Patrick. So what exactly is *The Avengers* all about?' Given sufficient time I might have written a lengthy treatise on *The Avengers*, but how was I to condense its many brilliant ideas, experiments and ventures into fantasy into a sentence?

'*The Avengers* is about a man in a bowler hat and a woman who flings men over her shoulders,' I spluttered. And with these words the deal was clinched—Patrick Macnee (Macnee and Cameron 242).

Absolute unreality, violence, symbolism, magic, masques, sex, change – everything that excites the imagination—Jonathan Miller (quoted in 'Good-Chap Sexuality').

I am told that, in 1927, a Louisiana lawmaker (haunted by the ghost of Pythagoras, no doubt) introduced into the legislature of that state a bill that would have made the value of *pi* equal to precisely three—Hollis Frampton (quoted in Lunenfeld 7).

The point of Frampton's story quoted above is that the very malleability of *pi* makes it useful for calculating circumferences, arcs and volumes. Attempts to legislate neatness against this surplus of meaning are rarely successful. Not surprisingly, the same applies to genres. The concept derives from the Latin *genus*, which in turn comes from the word for giving birth. Originally referring to kinds of people, often by class, race or family, it is less an abstract classification than a series of piecemeal resemblances. The significance of genre as a force determining textuality continues from Roman imitations of the Greeks to late Hollywood's taste for remakes and quotation, with realism judged against the social world *and* prior cultural representations.

Genres are about the interplay of repetition and difference, their organisation and interpretation by producers, audiences and critics. This can happen at the level of cultural production, scheduling, regulation and reviewing. There is enough in common between the components of certain texts to group them together, and enough that is different to make us want to experience more than one exemplar. This represents a continuity in the history of literary and screen genres: they relate to the cultural attributes of a population at a certain moment, sometimes as reactions to those attributes, and sometimes as sources of them (Hunter 215). Just as the expansion of print literacy held implications for the emergence of the novel, so technological familiarity influences the mixed genres of latter-day TV.

The Avengers stands out from its US counterparts of the time because it eschews conventional weaponry in favour of the extended and controlled body – the women and their martial arts – and the extended and controlled gentleman – Steed and his stick. And it blends genres: 'James Bond meet[s] The Perils of Pauline'. In short, the thriller is connected to satire. Identification with the protagonists through a unitary moral universe is displaced by sophistication and knowingness. Henry Jenkins classifies *The Avengers* as 'fairly generic spy stories' in the Blackman days through to mixtures of 'wit, fantasy, science fiction and parody' with Rigg. Macnee described it to a waiting US media as 'comedy, way-out, bizarre-type entertainment'. Contemporary critics often associated it with British satirical television. As we have seen, Clemens thought of it as 'a Doris Day comedy . . . no drugs, black people or social problems'. The French have puzzled over the science-fiction designation, because there it is regarded as espionage fiction. In compiling his reference work on sci-fi television, Roger Fulton throws up his hands: 'Taking a literal definition, *The Avengers* was not a "science-fiction show", but then neither was it a show to be taken literally' (Meyers 127; Buxton 99; Usher; Jenkins 289; Macnee, quoted in Lowry; Musel 'Violence' 14; Clemens, quoted in Sutcliffe 29–30;

Putheaud 12; Andrae 113; Fulton 24).

We could subdivide the series into its own narrative pattern: science fiction, policing, treason, loss of identity, and power-hungry élites operating across horror, fantasy, comedy, soap opera, special-event television, quality drama, the spy story, crime series, thrillers, the fantastic, melodrama, British film noir and auteurist text. *Vanity Fair* 1995-style files it under 'Gumshoes'. While official publicity called Steed a 'special agent extraordinary', the cast referred to their programme as 'the-arse-about-face show' ('The All-Star' 242; Donaldson 'Steed'; cast, quoted in Porter 41). The 'Game' episode sends

Patrick Macnee in 'Game', as per Sean Connery in Dr No

up the entire genre. It is about a group of characters driven by an evil mastermind to play board games with dilemmas that relate to their professions. The stakes are their own survival. Steed's game is *Super Secret Agent*, but he plays for Tara's life, not his own: she is being smothered by sand from an hourglass as play proceeds. *Super Secret Agent* calls for courage, strategy, cunning and speed. Steed must surmount a series of obstacles: a wrestler, a time bomb, the choice of one safe door out of six exits from a room, having to crawl down a metallic tube towards the camera as per Bond in *Dr No* (1962), and confronting six assailants at six-second intervals with a six-chamber gun that has a single bullet. He cheats, firing the pistol at the hourglass to release Tara. A more even fight ensues and they vanquish the opposition. *The Avengers* breaks the rules of genre as per Steed in that game.

Does such intertextual blurring devalue genre as a method of analysis? Or does *The Avengers* disobey the iron codes of genre while borrowing from them? Such texts do not imply that genres no longer exist; on the contrary, they demonstrate the centrality of genre as a sounding-board and point of resistance against which originality can be measured. Repetition offers dependable characteristics alongside the *frisson* of surprise that makes for distinctiveness, engaging and entertaining production executives and viewers. TV series are reliable thanks to the categorical processes of cultural production. Television is a bureaucratically organised regime of pleasure; bureaucratic in that it is systematically planned and run, pleasurable in that its products are clever permutations of the everyday and the spectacular. More than that, they are designed to capture audiences and deliver them, either to advertisers (in the case of commercial networks) or to ideas (in the case of public stations). Genres combine the office memorandum with the jazzy commodity. One offers standardisation, the other marketability. Hence the particular significance of how norms of conduct, types of protagonist, and both narratively charged *and* incidental commodities intersect in TV genres.

The British espionage genre originated in excessive chauvinism, and in some ways still resides there. Wesley K. Wark connects innovations in cheap popular fiction to journalistic and governmental campaigns of xenophobia, shifts in the formation of classes and the division of labour, and the emergence of British moral panics about foreigners and spying in the decade following the Dreyfus affair:

> The enemy could be the Jew, the foreigner, the not-quite gentleman, the corrupted, the bomb-throwers, the women. Why the day needed to be saved was very much a product of national insecurities that began to mount at the turn of the century. At their heart were fears about the pace of technological and societal change caused by the impact of the Industrial Revolution. In the wake of its manifold upheavals, traditional measures of the international balance of power were threatened and the domestic structures of government upset. (275)

Concerns about British sea power contribute to stories from the 1880s on about the spectre of invasion. A second boost to the espionage genre comes with the inter-war years and a third via the crisis of empire and industry after the 1960s, when governments can only do so much next to movements of capital that are as significant as the movement of armies, and it becomes clear that traitors within are as common as enemies without (Stafford 496; Wark 280; Schlesinger, Murdock and Elliott 81). The issue of invasion and the banality or eccentricity of civil service and military attempts to manage it is regularly taken up in *The Avengers*, along with technological change and associated social relations. This is the UK trying to come to terms with post-industrial shifts from the mechanical to the electronic and a fragile cross-class affluence. In legal terms, the state's monopoly on defining legitimate violence is delegated to the spy; in the spy movie and TV series, this delegation extends to the colourful characterisation of a new sexual innuendo and brutality.

The opening titles mark out *Avengers* seasons from one another, establishing the mood and generic placement of each series for the viewer and providing points of reference for the neophyte and the repetition of pleasure for the initiate. The Hendry and early Blackman series resemble a hard-boiled detective urbanism, the Rigg credits are sophisticated and knowing, Thorson twee, and Lumley/Hunt nationalistic and disco-ish. The mixture of Dankworth's haunting jazz horns with visually indistinct silhouettes characterises the early, hard-boiled years. The UK version of the Rigg–Macnee titles commences with a montage of close-ups and medium-two-shot stills. Rigg is in leather, frills and pistol, Macnee has umbrella, overcoat and hat. The second Rigg season, in colour, begins with a deep-focus shot of two glasses. Steed is shown on a sparse set holding a champagne bottle. Mrs Peel shoots the top off and foam spurts out. They wink at one another, pour the drinks, and clink glasses. We see the empties next to his bowler and her pistol. A cut takes us to a two-shot of their feet extended across opposite sides of a desk. He elegantly skewers a carnation with a swordstick and tosses it to her. Catching the flower, she walks over and seductively puts it in his buttonhole. They smile, and we see them in silhouette standing at ease. Commercial time. Throughout, the memorable theme music of Laurie Johnson gives an exciting beat and melody that complement the editing.

The sand, the phone, the absurd

Miss King fires

In keeping with North American broadcast executives' infantili-sation of their audience, the series was overarticulated there in a ponderous, double-coding voice-over that began each episode of the Rigg era. You can imagine the question being asked in schedul-ing conferences: 'What are they avenging, anyway?' The answer was given, each time: they 'avenge crimes perpetrated against the people and the state', in a voice that combined the narrational excesses of Joe Friday *and* Pare Lorentz; such off-screen heroics. This was deliv-ered over an additional sequence: a waiter staggers on to a vast chessboard, a dagger in the middle of a target inscribed on the back of his coat. The close-up on the dagger is followed by a wide-angle shot of Steed and Mrs Peel walking towards him from the diagonals of the board. Steed picks up the champagne carried by the dead man, while she puts a pistol into her black boots. After he has poured the drinks, they charge their glasses and walk off. Steed is central to the Tara King openings. Everything is floral, romantic and unspectacular: a field populated by suits of armour, carnations, Miss King's hyper-femininity and his approaching middle age. *The New Avengers* blends the three leading actors into a British lion coloured in with fragments of the Union Jack. The theme music commences as per the previous series, but a military drum-beat counterpoints this erect beast while bass guitar riffs offer a disco beat.

Whereas British production histories tend to situate *The Avengers* in the context of police genres, the Bond films, Quatermass and the fashion industry, to one US television historian it can be categorised as simply a sample from Vietnam-era espionage shows (there were close to 20 of them over the 1960s). And Vincent Canby's article after the first New York screening was subtitled, 'Another Secret Agent Arrives on Scene'. He derided its similarity to other series already on the air and in fact to old radio dramas. Four years earlier, the *Daily Mail* responded cynically to the producers' efforts to differentiate their programme from others. But even the *Spectator* had found something to remark on in the very first season. Hendry and Macnee seemed to turn 'superficially ordinary life into a nightmare' (Putheaud 12; MacDonald 196–7; Canby; Black 'Undercover'; P. Forster).

After the first three British seasons, the *Daily Telegraph* declared the series part of 'a strange new growth in television', a hybrid called 'farcical melodrama'. What had begun as a satire of police shows was now diminished by a surfeit of 'bloodless massacres, comic villains and wildly absurd plots'. In 'The Undertakers', a gauntlet-throwing scene was reminiscent of the high-melodramatic excesses of *Richard II*. Unsure of how to describe the programme, and especially what to make of Steed's professional status, the newspaper's television critic sought guidance from producer John Bryce and story editor Richard (son of H. E.) Bates. Bryce thought it surreal. On the other side of politics, the *New Statesman* took an Olympian left-Leavisite view, dismissing the plots' weightlessness and lack of sincerity as the 'smugness' of a musical comedy. Perhaps the series was really a children's programme for adults: depthless of feeling, ultimately resilient, and wryly limited in facial expression. (*Thunderbirds* sees Lady Penelope looking very similar to Mrs Peel.) The power of this parody spelt danger for conventional espionage fiction (Bryce, cited in Marsland; Hope; Banks-Smith 'Dash'; Raynor).

As my informant Alex of California put it, the blend of film noir atmosphere and exoticism makes the early *Avengers* especially interesting, for while noir is frequently about the evil of the ordinary, its visual qualities make the evil and the ordinariness mutually obscure, difficult to discern and analyse with precision. This series took the unknowability of that screen style and matched it with narrative implausibility. At the same time, there was an articulation with broader cultural trends, the pop tendency we have already explored that spoke to my free-associating informant Stuart of Brisbane as 'avengers and modernism, Carnaby Street, free love, Beatles'. Yes, complete with Dutch angles, worm's-eye shooting, hand-held camera, and stunning graphic matches for scene transitions (from burning moustaches to a smithy's pyre in 'The Town of No Return'). During 'Second Sight' Macnee peers into the camera from between Blackman's bookshelves. We see her talking back to him in a mirror behind the bookcase. Then he lies on the floor and four talking heads arc reflected upside down in a table. Cut to a view of them through a door peppered with variably sized designer-holes. The dialogue is an exposition by her on the science of optical surgery. Six men lean forward to shake Mrs Gale's hand via point-of-view shooting in 'The Gilded Cage', each one going out of focus as they approach her/the camera. When Steed and Mrs Peel arrive in the psychiatric ward of a military hospital in 'The Danger Makers', the first shot has her throwing a beret patterned as a target into the middle of an analyst's spot-lit couch. Relatively unmotivated by the storyline, the moment jumps out at the viewer. It is a statement of stylishness, a questioning of medical authority.

The Avengers certainly used recognisable procedures of detection. Classically, detection has involved the identification and defeat of wrongdoers through an application of reason to explain irregular, undesirable events. As figures of modernity, both villains and detectives lose their individual identities through cloaks of substitution, paradigm changes of costume, task, face, voice and history. Identity is assumed and discarded, in keeping with the self-actualising, transcendent subject who can move across time and space with ease. The villain and the detective depend on each other through an overarching third term: the law and its embodiment in the state, which one must elude and the other convince that justice be meted out. This nexus of 'spectacular violence and social vacuousness' leads critics of the crime genre to blame it for modelling anti-social conduct, heroising the capitalist state, or delighting in base consumerism. But for John of London, *The Avengers'* flamboyance was 'the last time in history when it seemed plausible that the British state was worth defending'. In France, *The Avengers* stood out to my informant Florent of Lille for its blend of policing, espionage and the fantastic in stories, performances and *mise en scène* by comparison with the dogged realism of its local contemporaries. It confirmed and popularised a British film surrealism that dated back to Humphrey Jennings (Westlake 37; Kerr 2; Morrison 21).

Unlike the grand amateurs, who intellectualise in order to uncover criminal cause, effect and identity, police detectives are often stolid, proletarian servants, simultaneously decent and rough. The 1970s series took this format. *The New Avengers'* opening episode, 'The Eagle's Nest', is a rupture from its forebears. Gambit mocks a hyphenated surname to its owner, avows his lack of a prep-school education, and, *Sweeney*-like, says to an assailant: 'When you tried to kill me, you threw away the rule book.' The all-action working man arrives to represent careerism in the secret service of his country, breaking the series' style as he does so. Such characteristics connect officers of the law to the quotidian, even as they appear to stand above it, ever-vigilant to deal with infringements of order. Partnerships, rather than utility-maximising individuals, are typical. This affective bond allows them to maintain a sense of self as they encounter situations that frequently bear no relationship to their own lives. As the police move into a case, they often become involved in its detail and its people: informers, criminals, business proprietors, the ruling class. The narrative generally involves the following: the law is violated, the state finds out about it, the heroes try to find out why and how this happened and who was responsible, they encounter informants (some useful, others dangerous)

Ambassador Brodny (Warren Mitchell) downs one in 'The See-Through Man'

and have initial struggles with the enemy, the villain is revealed and defeated in a fight sequence, and a coda restores equilibrium. In broad terms, this is an apt description of *The Avengers*, but they were never recognisably upwardly mobile until Gambit. Their indestructibility positioned them more among the folk heroes of British oral narrative: Rob Roy, Dick Turpin and Robin Hood (Kaminsky with Mahan 55–6, 61–3; Giles 68–70; Merlman 99–101).

Earlier incarnations of the series were determinedly vague about the characters' official status. In 'Death of a Batman', Steed is said to have investigated corruption in the army during the Second World War, a history that is also drawn on for 'Game' with Thorson, and he sometimes mentions 'the Ministry'. Kingsley Amis pointed dismissively to British 'highbrow critics' who imagined that the mystery over the Avengers' employer was a flaw in the plot line. To his way of thinking, it was a joke between producers and viewers that demonstrated mutual 'mental agility' (Amis, quoted in Buxton 99). For most of *The Avengers'* classic years, government is in off-screen space, kept from us, Dr Keel, Mrs Gale, Mrs Peel and their adversaries by Steed. He is the conduit who alone holds ideological and organisational keys to precisely what is being avenged, if always with a partial narrative view. Espionage is a form of life that involves making certain routine moves without asking why and without there necessarily even being a good reason in the wider scheme of geopolitics. The preliminary to each episode, so similar to Bond openings, is instructive. An unexplained, disturbing event, often involving pursuit and murder, takes place. Following, in some countries, a commercial break, this strange amalgam of ominiscient and restricted narration becomes a kind of file memo enabling Steed and the viewers to move on. He uses the end-point of what we have seen – say, the death of an agent – to prompt his partner to solve the puzzle.

Because they are underpinned by the authority of sovereignty, but without its day-by-day administrative trappings, the Avengers stand out from any personal ambition or motivation while also avoiding a bloodless attitude to individuals. The series is of the Cold War, but the 'fun' component of it the brightness and gaiety of the best of the West. References to ideological foes are rare and humorous. So when Steed categorises Russian voices as 'the other side' or 'our worthy opponents' in 'The Charmers', he does so with affection and warmth. Warren Mitchell's characterisation of Ambassador Brodny in 'The See-Through Man' is slapstick comedy; he is Steed's friend as much as his enemy. Mrs Peel says of the Eastern Drug Corporation: 'We know "you know who" lies behind *that* pseudonym.' After all, the Prague Spring saw sales of the programme to Hungary, Romania, Czechoslovakia and Poland ('Avengers').

The nicest deviation from classic detective fiction comes in the depthlessness of *The Avengers*: rather than seeking motivation through temporary occupancy of the criminal mind or a recon-struction of its psychic imbalances, perversities are simply dealt with when encountered. They are narrative information capable of turning pleasures into obstacles and vice versa, not hermeneutic clues to the repressed truth of wrongdoing. Nor does the team per-suade a court of law or any organisation that the truth has been established: they have executive power. When Miss King appears as Steed's fellow professional, and they work for a fully achieved administrative character in Mother (Patrick Newell), the series loses this concrete ambiguity that had so beautifully expressed the every-dayness of governmentality. Mother had been designated as a

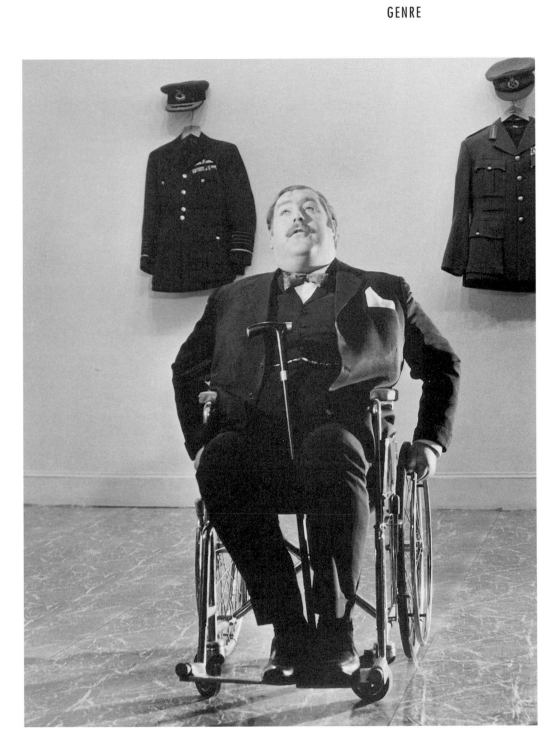

Patrick Newell as Mother

The demented escapee Burton (Griffith Davies) introduces us to 'The House That Jack Built'

Steed and Emma in the dark room

The developing paper holds the key

cameo in 'The Forget-Me-Knot', but audience reaction was so powerful in the USA that he was written into the remainder of the
series. That this was trumpeted in a press release, along with the
obvious links to M in the Bond saga and Alexander Waverly of
U.N.C.L.E., indicates the generic capture that American sales had
brought. For many contemporary critics, the export heroics of 1965
had been spoilt by the paradox of text-genre relations: standardisation displacing subtlety ('Meet'; J. Thomas; Billington). The USA
was a good place to get money and recognition – but you wouldn't
want those people telling you how to make television, now would
you?

To give some sense of the passage between genre and text and
back again in the series, I want to engage in an extended exegesis
here on 'The House that Jack Built'. As noted above, it fits into a
group of episodes that see either Blackman or Rigg isolated from
Steed for the bulk of the narrative, under highly personalised and
psychotic threat from a man in a remote house: familiar territory to
followers of both *The Avengers* and the horror genre. At the same
time, the episode in question varies considerably from the common
sexism of woman-as-victim/man-as-voyeur, even as it draws on
both those sources.

The foretitles show a man escaping from gaol and entering a
large country house. In the episode proper, Emma walks into
Steed's apartment, where he is developing film. She must break
their lunch date to explore a house left to her by a relative she has
not previously heard of: Uncle Jack. We cut to Mrs Peel's leather-
gloved hand starting up her sports car, with the key to her bequest
attached to the ignition key. Steed discovers after she has gone that
this key (which she had temporarily put on his photographic
paper) has left a mark. When developed, it signifies 'electronic
properties'. He telephones Emma's lawyer, who allegedly told her
about the legacy but expresses ignorance of any such communication or the supposed inheritance. Suspicious, Steed asks his friend
Pongo to check up on her. Thus far, we might be in a conventional
thriller; the fix is in for a woman to walk into a trap sprung by the
financial power of a mysterious man and then be saved by another
man via his agent. Two complications exist, however; the pre-credits diegesis, which is difficult to place within the story, and the fact

Mrs Peel enters
'The House That
Jack Built'

The oddities begin

The TARDIS-like orb

that the agent's name calls up comedy rather than the seemingly relevant genre.

The next sequence finds Mrs Peel in a two-piece white trouser suit with a double-breasted jacket covering her T-shirt, driving the Lotus down in the country. The car radio fails. A pudgy, bespectacled wee man in a Boy Scout's uniform walks out on to the road and asks for a lift. He shares with us that he had positioned himself precisely three feet beyond the car's stopping capacity, establishing an anality rarely seen in the post-war era. We get several reverse shots of him from behind the electronic key, which sets off photocells to create diversions for anyone following them. Emma drops him at the front gates and drives up to the house. Once the electronic key has left it, the car radio works again (it plays modern jazz).

She enters the house, inspecting an armoured knightly mannequin. Puzzled by strange creaks and the sound of a child's music-box, her face registers growing apprehension as she catches up to the less-restricted narration available to us. Extreme close-ups of stuffed owls reference *Psycho* (1960). Outside, the Boy Scout is at the door. Mrs Peel finds paper that shows someone has been practising her lawyer's signature. We cut to a ringing telephone. She picks it up, but no one is on the line. Meanwhile, the Boy Scout has entered the house. Emma pulls out a gun and hears a scream from the distance. Opening a door, she finds herself inside a different time–space continuum from the stately country home: the *mise en scène* of *Dr Who*. She has entered the Tardis, complete with an orb-like, revolving luminescent shaft, surreal *oubliettes*, and concentric circles. We return to Steed. He is told there has been no report from Pongo and decides to investigate personally. Space is left for the insertion of a commercial, with the text poised for Macnee to rescue Rigg from her mysterious assailant/gaoler.

Back from the sales pitch, we find Mrs Peel in the Tardis. A weird throbbing sound pulses insistently within and without her. Her gun remains drawn, heightening the sense of anxiety. The camera tracks her around the room. She opens several doors, all leading to the same space. She appears wry and confident but alert. There is no panic to be seen by a surveillant character or TV spectator. And the look here is all-important, because time spent in the house has

Striding purposefully

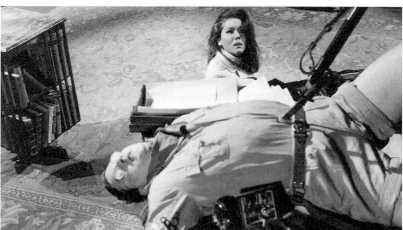

Pongo
(Michael Wynne)
penetrated

Mrs Peel encounters
her inner child

lacked any dialogue beyond her occasional, unsuccessful interpella-tions. The ante is upped via repeated extreme close-ups on her face, revealing a developing frustration. Canted angles increase the dis-placement for the audience as well as Mrs Peel, conveying the fact that our fuller sense of the narrative is nevertheless also incomplete. Yet she remains ready to inscribe rationality. As more and more doors lead to identical sites, she marks one of the orbs with a cross to identify it; she does so with her lipstick, a nice writing medium that connects logic and gender even as it locates us next to Greek mythology and Theseus's triumph over the maze and the minotaur. Then she walks up to and virtually becomes the camera, followed by a cut to a point-of-view shot from her perspective. More doors are tried, eventually leading back to the marked orb. The noise now includes growling and laughter, a disturbing mockery that emanates from some space of superior knowledge rather than an identifiable physical source or person. We are given two series of canted extreme long shots to re-establish scenes that bracket her reaction: 'Who is it? Who is there?' These are the only words spoken for 21 minutes, other than Steed's telephone conversation and her interior monologue. *On network television.* The wind blows and Emma discovers a Boy-Scout button before tripping over a rod. Panic is setting in, as we see her running via extreme close-ups. She finds herself in a room with a spiral staircase in place of the cus-tomary orb, and hears laughter. She descends the stairs, a man's feet in pursuit. The camera tracks her movement towards a window. What should be relief leads to despair: it is a small opening very high up in the building. Momentarily spun into medieval fantasies of the lady in distress in the château, we are returned to the Tardis. She fingers her gun and the camera follows her, focusing on her zip-up leather shoes. The music-box sounds again. She recognises the study and, opening a door, is back at the entrance-way. Now she feels trapped, and kicks out. Seeing the Boy Scout pinned to a desk by a bayonet, she pours a restorative brandy.

At this point, we move directly into Emma's interiority through a dialogue with a split self: 'I'm being watched. Every move I make, someone is watching.' She rejects any accompanying desperation. 'No. Reason it out,' she says, returning to the brandy. 'Reason it out,' again. She realises there must be a mechanism that rotates the

*'An exhibition
dedicated to the Late
Emma Peel'*

*Note the father
figure's head gear*

Adult, toy, machine

house each time she opens a door. Sounding out her ideas has worked: the set moves in response to door knobs being turned. In a brief cut to Steed, we find he is on the way and has successfully negotiated a detour, but at the price of burst tyres.

Meanwhile, Mrs Peel has found some control panels. She enters a room with a sign reading 'Welcome to an exhibition dedicated to the late Emma Peel'. Opening a doll's house, she recognises it as her own childhood possession and then encounters other family memorabilia: parental photographs, a doll that she clutches to herself, smiling, and a picture of her with her father wearing a Steed-like bowler. A voice speaks from an illuminated mask in an unpleasant tone, announcing she will find her questions answered in 'Section Four'. Making her way around the room, she sees old newspaper headlines about Emma Knight (the future Mrs Peel) inheriting her father's company. The sense of high finance is aided by ticker-tape. A sound recording plays, detailing her ascent to management of the firm and the decision to fire an automation expert: 'I couldn't agree with his methods . . . replace man with machine, subjugate him to it.' And so Professor Keller was dismissed. Back in what for want of a better word we might call 'real' time, she proceeds to Section Five of the exhibit – a witness to her own posthumous commemoration in a postmodern museum of interactivity – screaming Keller's name at a television screen. The male voice criticises her, insisting that mechanisation surpasses human endeavour. Now he will prove it. There will be no need for violence to make the point; she will be incarcerated and controlled, her will broken by a home that predicts her every move. This home will cherish her in a physical sense, but ultimately send her mad. She will commit suicide because the imprisonment is inescapable.

As if to underscore this hermetically sealed, solipsistic world, Emma now confronts blown-up life-size head shots of herself. She slashes diagonally across the panel of pictures, slicing through this power-mongering representation and showing the ability to do what in the horror genre could perhaps only be done *to* her: cutting her own image to pieces. She has entered the deictic, the 'this is here and now, that was there and then' sense of temporality. No longer acted upon, Mrs Peel is now utilising knowledge to gain some mastery over time and place. Stepping behind the huge

*A multi-media,
interactive museum
experience*

*Mrs Peel
slashes codes*

*The patriarch revealed
— Michael Goodlife as
Professor Keller*

She meets the mad
thing. Is there a
way out?

Steed arrives but
is he needed?

Emma's ingenuity
solves her dilemma.
'The House That Jack
Built' is no more

posters, she peers back out through the cut-up portrait of her face. Suddenly we see the feet of the man who has been pursuing her. She thinks it's Keller, but our fuller information suggests that this is the mysterious escapee from the pre-credits sequence. They fight. He is clearly unhinged, reciting nursery rhymes: 'The House that Jack Built' tropes the title of the episode. An extreme close-up on his eyes concludes the sequence. It is time once more for a commercial.

Returning from the refrigerator and our choice of sustenance, we find Steed nearby. He sees Emma's Lotus. Inside the house, the mad thing has a gun pointed at her. She outwits him and then locates the major control room. Keller's embalmed body speaks to her. She shoots at it. Outside, Steed approaches the car and switches off the radio. Back in the house, a recording has Keller telling her that he used his last year alive after diagnosis of a terminal disease to transform this built environment into a living device, one that transcends humanity. Unable to feel, it has no breaking point, no room for insanity; but it can speak and respond. Equipment panels light up and a synthesised voice engages with her queries. A world of imitation and deception is also there, playing with her imagination and fear. She sees a lion leaping at her and shoots at what is merely an image. This is almost a direct affront to her voiced belief of seconds before that 'I *can* reason it out.' The living madman, with us once more, laughs as if to show what awaits her. Then we get a montage of light and noise. Emma holds her hands to her ears, now comprehensively frightened. We cut to Steed, still outside. Help is on its way, but the interesting double question is: conventionally, will it be in time; and less obviously, will she need it? Mrs Peel hears a car horn; there is life beyond her prison, conscious life that knows she is trapped and is communicating with her. She struggles again with the madman, who gets caught in the suicide chamber of deadly gases that is the final option constructed for her. Using a hairpin, she pushes powder from her gun that she has attached to the electronic key down a hole in the console where computer cards react to her questions. The machine segment of the house explodes. Steed, by now inside the building, arrives in time for the orb's glass to shatter. But her ingenuity has solved the problem. He is its witness, and so are we: to lipstick, hairpins and rationality.

6 *The postmodern*

I love looking back through a photo album and, in a sense, *The Avengers* is like that. I see this younger version of myself, and I think, 'She's OK'—Diana Rigg (quoted in Rosenthal 12).

The authors wish to apologize for the confusion that has arisen over David, King of Scotland. Although one source claimed there had been a King David VII, subsequent checking proved this to be unfounded. However, the following points have been established with regard to the relationship of Patrick Macnee's Huntingdon ancestors and the kings of Scotland—Patrick Macnee and Marie Cameron (298 n.).

If you were an expert in any field, the last thing you'd want was a visit from Steed or Emma. Invariably just before or after a visit from the Avengers, said expert would snuff it—Dick Fiddy ('In' 13).

The postmodern is many things to many people. It is often taken to include an aesthetic style, in architecture or novels for example, that tropes or quotes other forms in a *mélange* of cultural features; an historical template, designating economic adjustments towards internationalism and a turn by industrialised countries away from manufacturing in the direction of services; a philosophical discourse that deconstructs existing forms of knowledge by using their own precepts to undermine them; forms of identity politics that go beyond constitutional and class bases for defining political agency; the decline of power by the major forms of social reasoning that have dominated the past century (liberalism, Marxism, psychoanalysis and Christianity); the break-up of big government; and a series of cultural theories derived from and informing any and all of the above. John Clarke's assault on the postmodern is entitled

Diana Rigg
encounters difference
('Small Game for Big
Hunters')

'Enter the Cybernauts,' troping *The Avengers*. He criticises a loss of serious narrative in both aesthetics and politics. Overlapping and contradictory semiotic systems confuse rather than clarify our comprehension under postmodernity: *too much* meaning has been generated. In TV terms, the postmodern deposits us in a superfluity of screen palimpsests that are excessive for the needs and capacities of a single story.

This resonates with numerous *Avengers* episodes. 'Small Game for Big Hunters' commences with the sound of hand-beaten drums and a wilderness image. A man is flailing about in water, anxious as if he were being hunted. War cries can be heard off-screen. Skulls are in the trees and the man holds a machete; but to no avail. He is shot in the back with an arrow. Then the camera closes in on a signpost. It is 23 miles from London. This sequence is about the shock of disconfirmation, an uncertainty that generic pointers, or even deictic experiences, provide adequate knowledge. After the main titles, Mrs Peel responds to Steed's description of the dead body: 'We're not living in a primitive country. This is Hertfordshire, England.' In the Gale episode 'Death of a Great Dane', the opening shot is of flowers next to a loudspeaker playing music. We are in a graveyard, with a minister performing a service and a Great Dane among the mourners. The minister consoles a grieving man, and the camera pans to a sign indicating that this is a pet cemetery. 'The Gravediggers' also commences in a cemetery. A funeral march accompanies a burial. The mourners leave and a gravedigger does his job. When all are gone, the camera zooms in on the freshly turned sods. They are moving. An aerial appears through the ground, disturbing us as well as the turf. The titles come up. Much later, we learn this is a telescopic solar cell designed to jam the nation's early-warning protection against missile attack. 'The Living Dead' commences with an establishing shot of a coal mine: industry. It cuts to a sign outside a pub that reads 'The Duke of Benedict': countryside. An old drunk buys a bottle, stumbles out, and makes his way to a graveyard. A headstone is rolled back to reveal a white-coated man who emerges and walks slowly off. A reaction shot shows fear on the drunk's face. We cut to the pub and the church. A bell tolls, pulled by the disinterred figure. The drunk tells people that the duke's ghost has returned: horror. Then the titles

Boffins gone bonkers – 'From Venus with Love'

appear, with a punning conundrum for the viewer that matches these generic and diegetic mixes: 'Steed finds a Mine of Information/Emma Goes Underground'. Along the way, efforts to unveil an alternative subterranean world set up as a preliminary to taking over England are complicated by the rivalry between two investigators: FOG (Friends of Ghosts) and SMOG (Scientific Measurement of Ghosts).

The same dilemma/pleasure of knowledge/ignorance characterises 'Death at Bargain Prices'. The opening master shot is of a quite empty London street. Big Ben strikes. Then we cut to a department store, presumably after hours, and a medium close-up of a man among some toys. He calls the lift, and goes down four levels. From his point of view, we watch the lift halt between floors. Then he goes up again and exits. A large plastic Yogi Bear toy waves at him. Another man comes out from behind it, shoots him, and walks away. After a close-up on an extremely wobbly Yogi, the titles appear. Commercial break concluded, we are returned to a truly busy street and the store. A toy elephant advances on Steed in close-up, complete with umbrella. Mrs Peel is trying on a pair of gloves. Moving on to the maternity section, they are mistaken for a couple. Emma is critical of the store because the china is mis-catalogued. At the end of the story, with London about to be destroyed by a nuclear device, we return to this space to find that Steed has '[c]ome for my teddy bear. Can't sleep without one.' Confronted by the villains of the piece, he fires ping-pong balls at them from a toy gun. In menswear he poses as one of several mannequins. In sporting goods, a cricket bat is redisposed as a weapon, he swots away a knife and deposits it at the centre of a dartboard. Faced with a firing squad at the conclusion to 'The Living Dead', Steed is offered a last request. He asks: 'Would you cancel my milk?' Emma machine-guns the executioners and he kisses her lightly on each cheek. They debate the cliché nature of a plot device in 'The Danger Makers'. She explains her escape from capture by knotting sheets together and climbing out of a window. He mutters, 'Oh, that old thing.' Her retort is both commonsensical and metatextual: 'Originality didn't seem important at the time.' This is postmodern irony, generated by scrambling signs to do with genre and gender.

While *The Avengers* certainly did fracture stories, sometimes knitting them into other ones, sometimes restoring an equilibrium from different diegeses, and often making style *into* content, this always touched on political questions. That is the good side to the postmodern: its taste for citation sooner or later gets around to conflict. Consider the comment on the fate of experts mentioned in the teaser to this chapter. Applied intellectuals do suffer in the series: boffins are often portrayed as good men in white, doing the work of bringing Britain into the modern, but their efforts are all too frequently perverted by a subversive organisation or their own will to power. The split between the modern project of seeking truth and control through the efficient and effective use of knowledge and the idea of ratification through democracy, is critical. Paradoxically, then, the series was all about common sense in place of the grand narrative of scientific progress. As publicity materials carefully pointed out, there was 'nothing of the intellectual about Patrick Macnee, although he is a voracious reader of newspapers and international magazines' ('Profile').

All professional people are suspect. In 'Immortal Clay', an industrialist explaining the development of an unbreakable plastic dismisses Mrs Gale – 'I don't approve of amateurs' – while the evil plotters of 'November Five' are connected to an image-centred public-relations concern. This is satirised by having Macnee write speeches for Blackman to deliver. The reversal of authority and scrambling of signs is central to 'The Little Wonders', which is about an international gang of vicars and bishops who carry guns, have their annual meeting seated at tiny desks in a primary school, and form a Commonwealth Mafia called 'The Bibliotec'. The membership includes Fingers, the vicar of Toowoomba. They are gunned down by Lois Maxwell (of Miss Moneypenny fame) with a semi-automatic weapon secreted in her nurse's cape. 'Escape in Time' stages different periods of British history into which twentieth-century felons are allegedly able to move via a time machine. You might choose the Restoration, Georgian England, or the Edwardian era as places to start anew (the latter is exemplified to prospective clients via the insertion of a Latin American dictator into footage of Derby Day at Epsom in 1904). The absurdity is emphasised via a strange assortment of location shooting for one action sequence (where Emma is pursued by a man on a motor bike dressed in equestrian costume) and the stagiest of sets, something from a Gene Kelly dance scene. The overtness of the conceit is heightened at every turn, drawing the viewer's attention to the artifice in ways that, in concert with the playful racing documentary, help to problematise more realist sequences. Mrs Peel rolls up her newspaper and pretends to use it as a telescope, the barber on the street is Sweeney Todd, escorts wear saris, cardinal's uniforms or cricket blazers, and the acting atmosphere is pantomime Arthur Askey- or Ian Botham-style. The time travel itself is a parody: the dates are set by a fruit machine.

The dangers of expertise and a headlong rush into rationality, efficiency and effectiveness are probably best remembered in the Cybernauts trilogy, stories that range across both Rigg seasons and on into the *New Avengers*. 'The Cybernauts' commences with the mysterious murders of numerous top businessmen. The cause is the dastardly creations of a former government inventor, Dr Armstrong, who designed robots capable of clearing radioactive debris.

Lois Maxwell
(Sister Johnson)
attends the needs of
David Bauer (the
Bishop of Winnipeg)
in 'The Little Wonders'

Steed hears Cathy's
confession
(The Little Wonders)

'Escape in Time' finds Steed exchanging toys for freedom

Along the way to uncovering the plot, we are offered meditations on the desirable condition and interaction of economy with society and polity. Steed infiltrates the United Automation Corporation, determined to prevent men and women from having their jobs taken by new technology because of the social cost. Dr Armstrong waxes industrial on the superiority of his innovation over workers: 'This is the age of the push-button. . . . The machine . . . is obedient . . . and more competent . . . a perfect, trouble-free labour force. . . . Today we have machines that not only work, but think.' His criminal activity revealed, Armstrong uncovers the political component to his vision of the future: 'government by automation' is 'the only solution'. But this is also a dialogue, very much after the Bondian model, where the evil mastermind attempts verbal seduction of the hero, who is meant to be converted and overwhelmed. And Steed's half of the system produces an unusual seriousness and reflexivity: 'I'd say that's up to the voters.' He expresses clear opposition to 'a cybernetic police state'.

In search of distraction during the Gulf War, *New York Post* TV critic David Bianculli turned to the early Blackman–Macnee episodes on A&E. But a particular dialogue about the futility of the arms race, early-1960s style, was so prescient that he could not relax. The issues were still real ones. As Raymond Durgnat had put it a quarter of a century earlier, Blackman was simultaneously 'a potentially Hawksian heroine' and 'a highly emancipated girl in leather . . . i.e. she's the near future'. The *Sunday Telegraph*, by contrast, had bemoaned the series' focus on 'clothes and gadgets and other self-conscious trimmings, and nothing on the thing that matters most of all, the book'. The displacement of narrativity by gloss, and the dangers of totalising expertise, characterise both the series and the postmodern. To TV theorist Jonathan David Tankel, '*The Avengers* became the perfect international television programme: in its historic time, it was simultaneously all things to all people and nothing at all' (Bianculli 'Sexy'; Durgnat 184, 104; Purser 'Thoughtless'; Tankel 88).

Emma tries to program while Steed intervenes physically in 'Return of the Cybernauts'

'Look (Stop Me If You've Heard This One) But There Were These Two Fellers', who are Jennings (Julian Chagrin) and Maxie Martin (Jimmy Jewel)

Thorson in Rigg hair and John Cleese as Marcus Pingham in 'Look (Stop Me If You've Heard This One) But There Were These Two Fellers'

Steed and Mrs Peel confront some stereotypes in 'The Gravediggers'

One of the first Rigg episodes, 'The Master Minds', has the final fight sequence shown in silhouette only, behind a film screen in a school hall. In the last season, 'Look (Stop Me If You've Heard This One) But There Were These Two Fellers' celebrates a passing world of popular culture. Acting on instructions from a Punch and Judy show at Vaude-Villa HQ, two clowns murder developers who are planning to pull down old theatres. Each corporate man is disposed of in the genre of slapstick, via the banana skin, for example, and a joke-writer is found dead in a pile of his own one-liners (Ironside). The finale to 'The Gravediggers' has Emma tied to miniature railroad tracks (vertically down the line, since their span is so tiny) while Steed struggles with the evil driver to save her from decapitation-by-toy. We lose diegetic sound in favour of a silent film piano accompaniment/Dudley Do-Right cartoon theme, as the film speed increases. 'The Hidden Tiger' is about a conspiracy planned by PURRR, the Philanthropic Union for Rescue, Relief and Recuperation, which creates 'identicat' pictures to find lost pets. Ronnie Barker plays Edwin Cheshire, who slurps milk for pleasure. Other employees include Dr Manx, the inventor of 'psycat therapy', and his lover Angora, who is made up with feline eyebrows and shadow. PURRR's Furry Lodge is filled with cat icons: huge sculptures, cutout signs and small figurines. Steed's putative lost pussy is 'Emma . . . cuddlesome brown tabby'. (Told this by him after the event, she

'The Hidden Tiger' is a pussy cat that stands between Steed and Edwin Cheshire (Ronnie Barker) of P.U.R.R.R.

purrs.) Her imagined pet is 'John'. He has 'aristocratic' features and is 'very bad-tempered first thing in the morning, until he's had his first glass of champagne'.

The postmodern is a mannered approach to life that fetishises the future and celebrates ditching the past and the truth, a sophistication that is determined to avoid looking surprised. When the past is visited – Steed donning Edwardian attire and *politesse* – the postmodern text drips with irony. As he smilingly puts it in 'The Charmers', 'I haven't killed anyone all week.' Emma responds to being confined to a cell in 'The Living Dead' by doing a handstand against the wall. She overpowers her gaoler, knocks him and another man out of action, and then smiles into the camera in close-up. 'The Hidden Tiger' also draws attention to the artifice of film in a sequence with Steed and the eccentric Major Nesbit, a former big-game hunter. The scene opens with a point-of-view close-up of a lion charging the viewer. The major provides a voice-over. He is in pith helmet and khaki, brandishing a rifle. The camera goes wide to reveal his film projector and the screen on which the charging animal has been shown. Then he points to its stuffed head, mounted on an adjacent wall. History again repeats as farce, the context altering its meaning, in 'Fog'. Steed and Tara engage with a Jack-the-Ripper figure who attacks delegates to a fog-bound conference on disarmament; the suspects come from a society dedicated to uncovering the identity of the Gaslight Ghoul, a mass murderer from 1888. Here we see some fascinating paradigmatic substitutions: prostitutes are displaced by pacifists, and those bizarre late twentieth-century figures – *afficionadi* of the serial killer – are part of the phenomenon they study. The interdependence of binary opposites is everywhere: in the words of *The Avengers Annual* for 1967, 'Emma Peel plays mod to Steed's trad' (*Annual*, quoted in Chibnall), staging a meeting of the present future with the present past.

This explains why they must never actually make it sexually. To do so would be cliché. Umberto Eco:

> For me the postmodern attitude is that of a man who loves a woman who is intelligent and well read: he knows that he cannot tell her, 'I love you desperately,' because he knows that she knows (and she knows that he knows) that that is a line out of Barbara Cartland. Yet there is a solution. He can say, 'As Barbara Cartland would say, I love you desperately'.
> ('Correspondence' 2–3)

As Macnee has said, reflecting on his acting style, 'I'm a good sub-Rex Harrison or David Niven.' Everything has been said before. All the permutations can be predicted, so the speakers must make metalinguistic moves to avoid boredom. They can only keep the excitement alive in the spectator by avoiding the declaration or consummation of feeling; hence the longer life of *The Avengers* and *Gunsmoke* than *Moonlighting* (Macnee, quoted in Kelly; Kozloff 76). Endless deferral perfects limerence; as C. Lee Harrington and Denise D. Bielby have suggested with reference to soap-opera vicariousness, perhaps this is about falling in love with the love of others (137), subject in this case to a further displacement into knowing it could have been perfect but not actually proceeding.

Jesse Carr-Martindale, creator of *Dempsey and Makepeace*, preferred that series because *The Avengers* was 'a pastiche . . . something not quite real'. Precisely. Its focus on the bizarre and the improbable provides weightlessness to the principal characters, lifting them beyond the contingencies of time and place that mark out

Steed with the young and the moronic

naturalism and realism. Looking back on the series 25 years later, Thorson explained its retro-appeal very much in terms of the 60s as a mythic time when fashion, music, colour and pleasure worked together to transcend the given stuff of life. That looks good to bearers of the despondent social fabric of the 1990s. More than nostalgia, it provides tools of stylishness, of choreographed, ironised violence. And its mixing of generic conventions plays with the spatial resonances of popular fiction, pointing out their arbitrariness in the process: a hospital doubles as a high-technology manufacturing plant, an abandoned mine hides an alternative universe, there are subterranean takeovers of Britain, and an observatory society is plagued by ophthalmology mania. (Regardless, the makers of *Dempsey and Makepeace* were so unaware of world TV history that

they cast a Captain Kangaroo lookalike as the head of police opera-
tions.) (Carr-Martindale, quoted in Hodgson; Green 109; Chibnall;
Thorson, cited in Bassom 64; DeAndrea 88).

'Dial a Deadly Number' places Steed in a stockbroker's office. A
recent exchange is referred to as 'quite a killing' while the camera
moves to a mounted fish eating another fish on the wall of a bar
where waiters regularly make share-price announcements. When he
arrives at a dressy dinner party, the *Avengers* theme music plays
diegetically as muzak. Later, two motor-bike riders speed towards
him; Steed executes a mock bullfight manoeuvre with his coat.
Then he embarks on a pseudo-duel with his chief adversary that
finds them walking back-to-back away from one another, the con-
test conducted over guessing the vintage and grape of the wine each
is drinking. Mrs Peel uses her compact during a meeting about
share prices to see who is coming in behind her. The finale has a

*An Orientalist
moment from 'Small
Game for Big Hunters'
with Col. Rawlings
(Bill Fraser) and Lala
(Esther Anderson)*

seemingly vanquished villain finding a gun and firing it – but he only succeeds in shooting the cork off Steed's champagne bottle, which ricochets on to his own head. In each case, postmodern irony is deployed: the conceit is to take an aspect of hierarchical social structure or culture, or a serious generic convention of screen drama, and deflate it by forming a syntagmatic relationship to the series itself, either intertextually or as a commentary on middle-brow culture. 'Small Game for Big Hunters' mocks the British colonial past, specifically a rejection of African peoples' right to self-determination and expulsion of their former conquerors from the mythic state of Kalaya. A particularly pompous professor shares with us his Renaissance-man capacity to transcend the space between Occident and Orient. He is aware that the 'European mind is a literal one; it requires logic', while time in the 'Far East' allows him to accept 'the inexplicable'. For his compatriot, a deranged ex-colonel, the way to engage in cultural dialogue is to 'Take 'em some coloured beads. Always helps.' But the recidivists' scheme to unleash deadly insects in the African state that expelled the British, and hence create a wave of new colonialism, is foiled by Mrs Peel, Steed and Lieutenant Ratsati of the Kalayan Intelligence Service, an Oxford-accented undercover agent. Such moves narrativize 'both the persistence of Empire in a British context and the fear of its resurgence in the future' (Mason 29).

'The Gravediggers' is set at the Sir Horace Winslip Hospital for Ailing Railwaymen, where nurses keep loaded guns under their uniforms, a box of flowers and a coffin are solemnly brought into the operating theatre, surgeons use blowtorches, and a patient's plaster cast conceals weaponry. The partners in deception are the local funeral parlour, whose slogan is 'Undertake with Decorum'. An eccentric retiree, Sir Horace, unwittingly funds and houses their illegal activities. Steed meets him at 'Winslow Junction', a replica of an English country railway station. To obtain entry to Sir Horace's house, people blow a whistle as if at a railway station. Steed and Sir Horace sit down to a meal on a mocked-up train ride, complete with painted scenes on a canvas that is pulled along before them to simulate movement, while a worker sways the carriage. Engine noise is on hand via an ancient phonograph. But unlike that other grand simulation of railway travel, *Night Mail* (1936), the rocking device is not there to herald the role of the worker in building Britain. Rather, it is a small inhibition to the sharing of brandy balloons, as Steed listens to Sir Horace: 'Railways made civilisation possible. Opened up the Wild West.' Even as he expresses concern that rail travel has been 'murdered by the motorcar', the magic of cinema and the artifice of romantic ruling-class fantasies are exposed in the nicest possible way. Then the two men leave simulation for the real thing in miniature. Sir Horace offers Steed a ride in the child's seat of his personal engine, 'John of Gaunt'.

The *Guardian* suggested in 1967 that *The Avengers* represented 'something more universal than the public and private lives of secret operators'. As per the passage of popular fiction into a seemingly timeless canon of elevating novels, the paper's TV critic imagined himself embarked on 'pseudo-scholarship, like a literary gent savouring the sensation of seeing Don Quixote suddenly blossom from a gimmick used to debunk phony romanticism to a literary giant'. *Stage and Television Today* attacked 'pseudo-intellectuals subjecting . . . [Steed to] sociological analysis' (Reynolds; Shakespeare). For Clemens, alterity was part of the programme's academic appeal:

> The sexual tensions are good. Under the surface *The Avengers*
> has been seen as a very Freudian show, with classic
> relationships touching the sadistic and masochistic. Most
> letters we get are from university dons and intellectuals who
> see through the innuendos. (Clemens, quoted in Short 11)

He says the makers of the series saw it running at two levels. For those who wished to concentrate on the story, it was strong, and there was this punning unoriginality for another kind of viewer (Clemens, cited in Vincent-Rudzki 11). I suppose I represent pseudo-scholars looking for postmodern intertextuality, where quotation is both integral to mood and story and incidental, redundant, an additional source of pleasure to people in the know without alienating those in search of the plot.

Pseuds are clearly addressed in 'Epic'. Emma is kidnapped by former film-makers in search of what would later become known as a snuff movie, with her murdered on screen in a variety of generic set-ups. The three villains trope several stellar figures who went

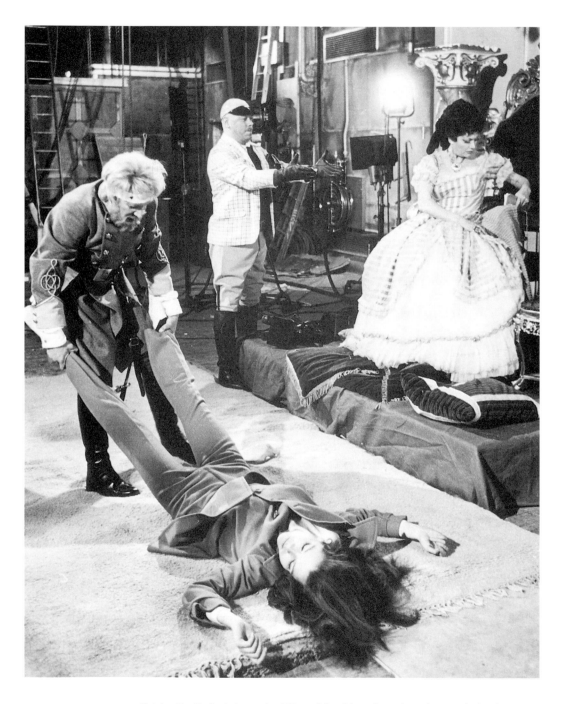

'Epic' – Mrs Peel is kidnapped to Z.Z.von Schnerk's studios, where she must deal with Stewart Kirby (Peter Wyngarde), von Schnerk (Keneth J Warren) and Damita Syn (Isa Miranda)

through a decline. Stewart Kirby (smoking jacket, drink, pipe and white hair) could be George Arliss or John Barrymore; Damita Syn (dark hair, pearls, cigarette holder and flapper gear) probably Lily Damita and Gloria Swanson. Z.Z. von Schnerk (Germanic accent, bald, black leather gloves, moustache, whip and cravat) is undoubtedly Erich von Stroheim. We open with posters of their old triumphs: *The Sophisticated Scoundrel* and *The Bad Bad Lady*, followed by a close-up on an Oscar look-alike. This is matched by music as per a 1960s epic. The episode title itself appears in lettering akin to the walls of Jericho. These imaginary films call up Swanson's *The Untamed Lady* (1926). The three are watching silent footage of Emma. Von Schnerk remarks on her 'animal vitality'. A sign tells us this is 'Schnerk Studios, Home of Z.Z. von Schnerk Productions'. We sense all three are enacting *Sunset Boulevard* (1950), with Mrs Peel as William Holden, entering with the plot already in motion and fated to perish.

Apart from this trivia guessing game, the episode makes stylistic reference to the artifice and apparatus of cinema. Captured and drugged, Emma wakes. Opening a door, she is confronted by cameras. Leaning on a wall, she tears through what is merely paper brick. Her kidnapping is then re-created, making the trope reflect the principal diegesis. She flees the set, emerging to the sound of church bells, wind, a bridal veil, and an invitation to her own wedding. She smirks at it. We learn that a fan is making the breeze. This looks like a horror film. The priest presiding is a ghost and the confetti turns into a storm. But it also resembles a dream sequence, with Mrs Peel walking about in slow motion. Shoved by the priest, she tumbles down a leafy glade. (Confused, as one would be in slowmo.) A bell chimes and normal speed is resumed, but now she finds herself at a funeral, complete with casket and a sign urging Emma Peel to rest in peace. Still in the churchyard, lights noisily flick on to illuminate the gravestones. Each one gives the same RIP message. The priest, defrocked, cuts a ghostly figure behind the wheel of a hearse, made up in hyper-feminine, clownish style. Mrs Peel runs to the empty set. The floodlights come on, with extreme close-ups on them, and on her, our attention drawn to the filmic process as much as to her interiority. She spots a dead man dressed as Steed, slumped in a director's chair with Steed's name on it. Time to move to another stage. A woman sits on a throne, knitting, as Alexander the Great enters. Emma laughs, the 1960s viewer to a Cecil B. DeMille epic who reads silent-screen realism as comic melodrama. But the spectator is rudely stitched into the text when Mrs Peel is described as Alex's 'wicked little sister'. They fight. She wins but is knocked out by her 'mother'. The director walks on to the set, camera in hand: 'mark it'. A clapperboard identifies the text as *The Destruction of Emma Peel*. She regains consciousness in a Western bar. Told by a cowboy to leave or face the consequences, she is involved in a gunfight, shooting her adversary. There are noises off and we see the director upstairs with his camera. He calls the event 'a compendium of all my films', full of 'passion' and 'danger'. A sign is inserted for us, reading 'Meanwhile . . . Back at the ranch'. This signals a different diegesis, outside von Schnerk's terrain: *The Avengers*. The ranch referred to is her apartment, where Steed is looking for clues as to her whereabouts. And so it goes.

Many other episodes borrow from and reference obscure and well-known texts, a citational feature of the postmodern. These thefts range from a four-line reference in a biography of the noted pathologist Sidney Smith about working with arsenic in a cemetery that provides the basis to 'Mandrake', and characters such as the gamekeeper Mellors from 'Silent Dust', evoking D. H. Lawrence's *Lady Chatterley's Lover* and Hardy Amies's 1961 spring clothing collection, to a whole raft of nicknames for old army men that resonate with Bulldog Drummond. My informant Colin, who spoke with Clemens about the series, suggests the Peel–Steed relationship drew from Bob Hope and Bing Crosby's *Road To . . .* cycle.

'Too Many Christmas Trees' finds Steed and Peel in the mansion house of a publisher so enamoured of Charles Dickens that each room is a tableau representing one of the novels; the Hall of Great Expectations comes complete with Miss Haversham and her cobwebs. At the Christmas fancy-dress party, Steed is cast as Sidney Carton and Emma as Oliver Twist. The other intertext, pushed by publicists at the time, is Macnee's recurring nightmares from his war service. They form the principal narrative problem of the episode. Mrs Peel, who has recently published an article on psychoanalysis, diagnoses 'childhood regression' (Donaldson 'Steed'). The recurring dream and its setting resonate with *Dead of Night* (1945,

From 'Epic'

Steed confronts villainy: Horatio Caine (André Morrell) and Farthingale (Allan Cuthbertson) from 'Death at Bargain Prices'

part of which was directed by Charles Crichton, director of 'Epic'). The finale has reflexive shots and a gunfight as per the hall of mirrors in *The Lady from Shanghai* (1948). It also contains a beautiful reference to *Goldfinger*. Steed and Mrs Peel are opening his Christmas mail. She reads a card aloud:

> *Emma:* 'Best wishes for the future, Cathy.'
> *Steed:* Mrs Gale! How nice of her to remember me. What *can* she be doing in Fort Knox?

'The Hidden Tiger' concludes with Emma freeing Steed from his bonds. Looking around at hundreds of milling cats, she offers 'pussies galore'. The first Emma Peel episode, 'The Town of No Return', eagerly awaited for comparison with Blackman, stole from *Goldfinger*. The opening of the film sees Connery emerging from water in frogman's gear, his head concealed by a stuffed fowl attached to the skull. He strips off to reveal summer evening dress underneath. The opening to *The Avengers* trope finds an amorphous figure appear on shore from the ocean. A large black plastic cover is unzipped to disclose a prim and proper English clerk, who approaches a watching crofter to request directions.

Steed's Second World War reunion in 'The Hour That Never Was' is held at Camp 472 Hamelin, troping the Pied Piper. 'Bizarre' draws on Evelyn Waugh's *The Loved One*. 'The Girl from A.U.N.T.I.E.' parodies both *The Girl From U.N.C.L.E.* and the BBC's nickname. Lewis Carroll's *Alice in Wonderland* and its bottle labelled 'Drink Me' are called up by the electronic key to the suicide room from 'The House That Jack Built'. In 'The Winged Avenger', Emma fights the enemy of the title to the sound of Laurie Johnson's version of the *Batman* theme, while 'The Morning After' (loosely based on John Buchan's *The Thirty-nine Steps*) finds Steed concluding a TV-watching session with 'Sock it to me', referencing an earlier episode of *Rowan and Martin's Laugh-In* that had concluded with Arte Johnson bidding 'Goodnight . . . *The Avengers*,' which was ending at the same time on another network. *Mission: Impossible* is called up by 'Mission . . . Highly Improbable' and *The Magnificent Seven* (1960) by 'The Superlative Seven', while Dashiell Hammett's *The Maltese Falcon* is a source for 'Legacy of Death' (Stern 3–4; Michael Richardson '1' 12; Cornell, Day and Topping *Guinness* 342; Donaldson 'Transmission'; Nolan). The toy train setting and farce-like style of 'The Gravediggers' follow on the Ealing Films tradition. 'The Gilded Cage' recalls *The Big Sleep* (1946): General Sternwood is the malicious Mr Spragg; Philip Marlowe's first meeting with his odd employer is recreated with Steed in a similarly exotic *mise en scène*. There is also a reference to the real, as Spragg is suspected of complicity in the Great Train Robbery. Anticipating her film appearance and borrowing from Fleming's *Goldfinger*, Cathy finds herself involved in a plot to gas Fort Knox.

Of course, it is possible to tumble so far down the path of pastiche that you enter self-parody, a charge that was levelled at the final series (Jackson). The dividing line is drawn at the point of viewing. Jon Pertwee's part in 'From Venus with Love' (another Bond trope) makes the point. He plays a Montgomery-like figure engaged in the Gestalt empty-chair re-creation of a Second World War invasion of Italy, using old-fashioned record players for sound effects and a reel-to-reel system taping his deathless commentary. Read it as you may. In 'The Charmers', Warren Mitchell as an amiable KGB man watches closed-circuit TV on a monitor located in the stomach of a female mannequin, who has a bandolier of bullets draped across her shoulder. In 'K is for Kill', a two-part *New Avengers* episode, a Soviet official solemnly awards Purdey the 'Little Mother of the Earth and Tractor-Drivers and Heavy Industry Award' for preserving *détente*. 'The Eagle's Nest' has a nice quotation from Sherlock Holmes, with Purdey listening while Steed tunelessly draws a bow across his violin. The grisly end to Cain in the cybernaut finale, when he is frozen in place, calls up an identical pose by the Tin Man in *The Wizard of Oz* (1939). John Garforth's novelisations of the series included *The Passing of Gloria Munday* (1976), a trope of the Latin tag *sic transit gloria mundi*. 'The Joker' has a shot of a man snooping through a hole in the wall as per *Psycho*. And in the pre-credits sequence to 'Silent Dust', Delius-like music overlays a vision of rural England, birdsong capping off the moment. But the referent suddenly switches to Hitchcock's *The Birds* (1963). The birds show fear or are dead, the music is overlaid with panic, and a scarecrow is found to be wearing a bowler. This is no idyll of an Albion beyond perfidy. A later reference to the estate as Manderley repeats the Hitchcock citation via *Rebecca* (1940). When Steed and Mrs Peel appear in boaters, cricket jackets (complete with quotations from *Macbeth*) Western-genre gear, a toga, and nineteenth-century costume inside a hot-air balloon, we are truly in an unstable story world (Nolan).

The Avengers itself became a source for postmodern appropriation. *The New Avengers* 'K is for Kill' episode has an early scene set in 1965. Steed rings Emma, who is edited-in from stock footage. The principal diegesis takes place 12 years later. He telephones again, addressing her as Mrs Peel. She reminds him that she's changed her name. He replies with a smile: 'Yes, I know; but you're still Mrs Peel to me.' The camera cuts twice to Purdey looking peev

Warren Mitchell as KGB man Keller in 'The Charmers', with Mrs Gale and objects de combat

ed and jealous. In *Some Will, Some Won't* (1969), Ronnie Corbett's office-worker drone imagines himself as a Bogart-style figure. Then, looking around the office, his eye lights on a hatstand. Reaching for a bowler and umbrella, he speaks as Steed, interpellating Tara. The early 1970s incarnation of *Doctor Who*, starring Pertwee, clearly troped Steed: Pertwee drove a vintage automobile, stood out in his clothing, and was accompanied by highly qualified professional women. Michael Richardson's genealogy of texts that borrowed from *The Avengers* stretches across the 1960s and 70s. It encompasses obvious examples, such as *Escapade* and *A Man Called Sloane*, as well as the noted cult comic *The Uncanny X-Men*, which takes the story of the Hellfire Club from 'A Touch of Brimstone' to rekindle Emma's role in *The Dark Phoenix Saga* of 1979–80. (In 1995, the ten-part comic-book series sold for US $15 a copy.) Macnee plays characters akin to Steed in a 1978 episode of *The Hardy Boys* series, the 1983 telemovie *Return of the Man from U.N.C.L.E.*, and the Bond film *A View to a Kill* (1985). He even appears in a bizarre episode of *Columbo* that pushes the limitations of fastidious espionage men as opposed to grungy, hard-boiled detectives: Peter Falk plays his customary role, on an ocean liner piloted by Macnee. Also on board is Robert Vaughn, whose character matches Macnee's elegance but adds secret corporate evil. Only Falk can provide the magical solution of working-class American savvy that uncovers this villainy. Clearly, the three roles depend on a sophisticated seepage from different series, an incipient quotation that is as important as the action (Thorburn 547–8).

'The Forget-Me-Knot' *Avengers* episode is ostensibly about poison darts that can force people to lose their memories; sure. It is really the exchange that replaces Rigg with Thorson, asking the *At last*

audience to transfer its affections. The end of Steed and Peel as a couple is signified by a newspaper headline that reads 'Peter Peel Alive. Air Ace found in Amazonian Jungle. Mrs Peel Waits.' This longing for the lost husband is countered by her wry comment to Steed: 'Trust him to make a dramatic reappearance.' He will be picking her up in a few minutes. It is time to part: 'Always keep your bowler on in times of stress. Watch out for diabolical master-minds. Goodbye Steed.' They kiss tenderly. Then we get the most intimate moment of the series, the masterstroke that finally over-turns British understatement. He uses her first name, while retaining the enigma of what went on between episodes and between the sheets: 'Emma . . . thanks.' As she passes Miss King on the stairs, Mrs Peel advises her on the mundane, the diurnal that their rela-tionship had always transcended: 'He likes his tea stirred anti-clock-wise.' The Bondian obsession with martini-making is domesticated by the conclusion to this least married of relationships. As Steed looks out from his window above, Mrs Peel turns and waves from an exact replica of his Bentley, driven by an exact replica of him. Peter Peel *is* John Steed. He could be represented in no other way. Emma's husband is a double of her partner. As Steed watches quizzically, she laughs at a joke that has been privately hers all along, just as the precise nature of their connection has been kept from viewers. The postmodern is just such a jokey troping that breaks up identity, certainty and knowledge. This is the figure in the jump suit who spoke to young Ian of Shepperton in the 60s, saying: 'You don't really think I'm taking this seriously, do you?' This is Emma Peel.

7 *Following*

The name of the nightclub was Le Stud, and the camera, ranging over the all-male audience, caught just a flash of the floor show – a half-clad dancing girl wrapping a chain around her body. In millions of British homes – even those in which the saucy name and symbolism went unquestioned – all was right with Saturday night. The Avengers were together again, as bafflingly platonic as ever, against some of the most civilized villains in the business—*TV Guide*, 1964 (Musel 'Violence' 13).

I had no way of knowing, of course, that all across America, other guys, dancing a seemingly endless tango with puberty, were equally bewitched. But nearly two decades since *The Avengers* avenged on prime time, I've run across men who appear quite normal until the conversation somehow turns to favorite TV shows. Then they smile, and their eyes gleam with bygone desire, and they mention *The Avengers*. And Diana Rigg—*Daily News*, 1987 (Cosgrove).

Back in the sixties all my class at school, boys and girls alike, fell hopelessly in love with Diana Rigg as Emma Peel in *The Avengers*.
   A beautiful woman who wasn't a wimp – now that was something special—*Daily Express*, 1984 (Paton).

There were very few fans until the late nineteenth century. The idea developed to describe followers of baseball when it emerged as a professional sport in the 1880s. They were thought to be sufficiently frenzied about their chosen teams to warrant a word of their own, derived from fanaticism. According to most contemporary research, fans construct parasocial or imagined connections to celebrities or actants. Fans of TV and music are subject to intense criminological and erotomaniacal evaluation. (And it must be said that to learn of the existence of 250 Engelbert Humperdinck fan clubs is to marvel at what people can love.) Chosen ones either fulfil the function of friends, or serve as spaces for projecting and evaluating schemas to make sense of human interaction. Eco teases out the issues in his exploration of what makes a 'cult' screen text. It is insufficient for audiences to adore the film or programme. They must also be able to domesticate the characters, removing them from the overall story and quoting their escapades and proclivities 'as if they were aspects of the fan's private sectarian world', a world opened up to other followers through quizzes and rankings. References to segments of an episode, or the typical behaviour of actants, become 'catalyzers of collective memories', regardless of their significance for individual plot-lines. Sequences and tendencies are disarticulated from screen time, reshaped and redisposed as part of the cult process. The seriality of TV makes this easier than the long form of film. The compilers of a volume on *Cult TV* subjected potential inclusions to four tests: if the series was old, could fans remember special qualities, tropes, or tunes? If new, did they cancel all other engagements to watch? Would they purchase video tapes and share recollections with like-minded others? And did it give rise to tie-in merchandising or fan-produced literature? (Leets, de Becker and Giles 102–4; Harrington and Bielby 102–4, 110; Eco *Travels* 198; Lewis and Stempel 8). We know the answers in this case. As Paul Gent has put it: 'For those of us who saw the original programmes, they will always conjure up that period of public and private life' (31).

Recent attempts by the professoriate to rehabilitate fans include numbering themselves among the group, lending academic textual interpretation a quaint demotic quality, licensing their own pleasures as professional acts of theory and critique, and claiming that the process is intensely risky, even academically death-defying. A vast array of conference papers, books and speaking fees suggests otherwise. For years, film intellectuals have traded on their immersion in texts, claiming 'the desire for cinema' as a high calling when it is as much a membership badge that excludes others. As Noel King has pointed out, this involves 'a regularity of critical description' cloaked in allegedly spontaneous efflorescences of adoration.

The routine generally requires taking a particular sequence or detail from a film and endowing it with representative stature politically or aesthetically. The typical cinéphile would negate such mundane specifications, claiming the passional as a critical alibi and underlining that this is 'uncontaminated by a relationship to television'. King argues against this by pointing to the specialist knowledge demonstrated by *Avengers* fans. After all, Hendry was kept on beyond *Police Surgeon* because of fan letters to ABC television: 'women cuddled their television sets' whenever he appeared, and the Controller of Programmes was initially opposed to the new Gale character because it was thought she would 'alienate female viewers'. The final series found Steed in a Rolls-Royce, because so many people had written in doubting that the Bentley could really keep up with the vehicles it was supposed to be chasing or eluding (Lewis 1; King in Willemen and King 227–9; Haining 189; Macnee and Cameron 206; Controller, quoted in Rogers *Complete* 37; Mansfield 24).

So perhaps telephilia lives. Monica Furlong, a critic for the *Daily Mail*, defined it 30 years ago:

> I suppose there is a moment in an addict's life when she sees where the habit is leading her, and could still give it up if she had the sense.
>
> The new version of *The Avengers* is beginning to make addictive demands on me.

Three decades on, Mary Houlihan-Skilton of the *Chicago Sun-Times* got more specific:

> In 1966, at the age of 14, I fell in love with John Steed. No, he wasn't the boy next door. And no, this isn't *True Confessions*.
> This is a 'television' confession.
> John Steed came from across the sea and swept me off my feet.

To these critics, it was 'the wittiest, wildest and kinkiest series on the air' (Bianculli *Dictionary* 38). Christophe Casa-Zza's confessions detail the career of '*un TV addict*', beginning with an eight-year-old's introduction to Emma Peel in the 60s. Faithfully tuned to each episode, and thinking of little else in between, his academic tastes turn from mathematics to literature because it promises romantic themes to match '*amour cathodique* [cathode love]', and he learns martial arts in order to be more like Emma. The author of *The Encyclopedia of TV Science Fiction* prefaces his book thus:

> I fought the Daleks (and won), thwarted the designs of THRUSH, did the Tracy air walk, pinned Emma Peel's picture on my wall (next to Fulham FC and the Stones), and later queued for Tara King's autograph when *The Avengers* came to film at my school. (Fulton ix)

Village Voice TV critic Bruce Eder has described Steed and Mrs Peel as basic trainers in sexual mores and, in the words of the *New Musical Express*, 'Anyone with a memory of the 60s television has *The Avengers* bound up in it.' Trekkies are the most prominent television followers from that era, with *Doctor Who* adherents a way back and *The Prisoner* somewhere in the mix. Their intertextuality is expressed in fanzines like *Rerun*. Its renowned cover features a composite figure comprised of Steed's bowler, Kirk's trousers, and the Doctor's scarf, *inter alia*. There can be difficulties in the relationship between fans and stars. The *Blake's 7* contingent welcomed Paul Darrow's presence at their conventions until he wrote a novel about his own character, which crossed the line dividing connoisseurship from entrepreneurialism. The nostalgia that is constitutive of television appreciation harks back to a lost era when fan, producer and text were in harmony. But it also delivers new and fantastic projections beyond what TV can sustain. Followers rewrite stories from the original series to meet their own politics (classically, sadomasochistic feminist interpretations of the Spock–Kirk relationship and efforts by queer fans to secure representation of their subjectivities on camera). Contemporary underground fiction explores the sexual ambiguities of Steed and Mrs Peel. Rigg's famous rejection of a London fan ('I'm sorry, but it's illegal to sign autographs in the street') was an ingredient in the mystique that placed her beyond TV acting: 'Fan mail baffles her – one doesn't get much at Stratford.' Rigg's mother often handled correspondence from gormless youths: 'My daughter is much too old for you and what you need is a good run around the block.' *Silver Screen* magazine became very anxious about her in the mid-70s. Following the demise of *Diana*, stories were run about her marriage that merged her with Emma Peel, asking how a strong woman could allow her career to be determined by a husband and blaming the new programme's failure on his jealousy. Future success, it was thought, depended on reworking her private life to match her most famous role (Cook; Gamson 230 n. 1; Jenkins 42; Tulloch and Jenkins 168–9, 239; Bacon-Smith 4, 35; Jenkins 175; Rigg, quoted in Musel 'En' 22; Rigg's mother, quoted in Smith 168; Miller).

For Thorson, some hyped-up suggestions made by fans in correspondence were 'frightening'. By 1969, two to three thousand letters were arriving each week and when she toured New York in the early 70s, a gay bar nominated her 'the woman we would most want to turn straight for'. Rigg reported with pleasure in 1993 that she was still receiving Queen of Sin postcards sent by fans for her signature, and Blackman reminisced chirpily to Channel Four about the days when she was 'invited to all sorts of strange parties and would I bring my whip?' In 1994, the Los Angeles-based Déja Vu company was selling autographed black and white photos of her ('Sexy in two-piece swimsuit') for US $30 (the same as a colour Matthew Broderick and five dollars more than a Bruce Willis or Isabelle Huppert). Throughout the series, Macnee received photographs from fans dressed in bikinis and negligées, along with an assortment of propositions. Years later he was recognised wherever he went. As Scottzilla, one of my ethnographically advantaged correspondents from Albuquerque, put it, 'I only remember thinking that Emma Peel was the only woman ever in the history of the world (other than Julie Newmar)'. The *Guardian* assured its readers that the 1990s video release would please the many 'men in their late thirties who can remember exactly where they were when, in 1965, Diana Rigg made her first incandescent appearance'. The passion and proprietorship with which people viewed the programme saw successive female lead characters 'in the unhappy position of a new wife who has supplanted an old one whom everybody loved' (Thorson, quoted in Short 11; Mansfield 27; Smith 173; Sweeting; Macnee and Cameron 222, 241; Salisbury; Déja Vu 2–3; J. Wilson; Melly

29 September 1968).

The psy-complexes were keen to visit *The Avengers*, especially after the grisly information that Myra Hindley and Ian Brady, the Moors murderers, were devotees of Mrs Gale's leather look. The efforts of clinicians to uncover its meanings were foregrounded in contemporary criticism. One writer confessed to being sent into a dream-like state. It forced him to suspend disbelief in the plots, while guaranteeing perfect recall after the event. British phenomenologists included it in research on viewers' reactions to programmes that broke with generic expectations: *The Avengers'* humour stood out, but its glamour and complex story-lines got in the way of some peoples' enjoyment. US viewers were promised that 'Freudian overtones, beloved of the British', would probably be eliminated in any co-production. Unlike most such analyses, however, this work was not so much concerned with discovering the evil done to young minds in the audience as it was dedicated to plotting and decoding the devices and materials that filled the screen. That drew a very stern reaction, nevertheless, from Ayn Rand, an early exponent of the active-audience position of contemporary TV studies, if without its prevailing politics. She was incensed by *TV Guide*'s contention that British audiences did not properly understand the show, misreading the satire decreed by its producers. This went against both a respect for viewers and the cardinal virtue of thrillers: that they engage audiences via heroism. Where the ironists producing *The Avengers* were stricken with 'an arrested modern mentality', their followers were able to abstract principles from the series to do with '*moral conflict*' (Teranko 83; Himmelweit, Swift and Jaeger 69–70, 78–84, 90–1; Lowry; Maurice Richardson 'On'; Musel 'Violence' 13; Rand 137–8).

This seriousness (along with the Freudian speculations about series followers) is played with in the bizarre 1985 fanzine, *With Macintosh, Life Saver and Hard Hat*. It refused to give a date, number, or contents page, pleaded with readers not to subscribe, and provided a centrefold pin-up of 'an *Avengers* fanatic' that showed a man and a woman, utterly without guile or style, carrying video tapes, fan books, beer and diet soda, and wearing Steed and Emma T-shirts. This was the follow-up to *With Umbrella, Charm and Bowler*, which lobbied for new screenings on US television. In 1969,

En Garde, a US 'personal-opinion-and-natter-zine' dedicated to the programme, had run a *Requiescet In Pace* section when the series ended its run, noting that the great legacy of the show would be Macnee's restoration of 'the Western world's faith in the English character'. It even had a conspiracy theory connecting the series to *The Prisoner*, based on speculation that Number Six was the missing Peter Peel and Tara an agent of the Village (her true affiliation given away by the penny farthing symbol on the wall of her apartment). By the mid-1990s, the series lived on in the West Midlands's *On Target – Stay Tuned* and Paris's *Le Fanzine* ('What'; *With*; *En*; Schultz 6; H. Davis 80; Fakrikian 'Chapeau' 41).

Some men who went through adolescence in the 1960s, like Mr D of Pittsburgh, rarely watched the show, precisely because their enjoyment of the Peel iconography was disrupted by the narrative drive: Mr D wanted the leather, its tightness on her skin, and her

Steed looks to Mrs Peel for truth

151

fighting abilities rather than the complex plots that provided the series' alibi. For later viewers, like Gareth in Wales, repertory screenings involved a complex negotiation of time commitments. In the days before off-air video taping became a standard part of domestic TV life, Gareth would run back from his music lesson to see a few minutes of Mrs Peel, sometimes leaving an audio-cassette player taping dialogue for later re-enactment with a cousin. To my informant Margaret of Manhattan, forbidden to enact violence-as-play by her upper-West Side liberal parents, Mrs Peel was the only powerful female character available for imitation in the games she played over summer with her younger brothers, games derived from TV drama. Despite this *frisson* of decadence, *The Avengers* could also be a family viewing experience for suburbanites, too. Michael recalls his 1966–8 domestic scene in Chicago and Pittsburgh as six people 'gathered around the tube chatting and guffawing over the quirkiness of it all'. For Jon in London, the episodes were playing out a subtle game of fashion transcendence, where class seemed to be gone beyond by the fantasy of dress-up; but Steed's aristocratic demeanour and connection to government showed where power truly resided.

The combination of exaggerated civility, casual violence and sexual subtlety, all accomplished on a spectrum of style, appealed to a broad cross-section of accepting and sceptical viewers. This is where the particular reading practices of followers really emerge. They conduct themselves like people who know 'everything' about motor cars. Fans do not resist the forces of consumer capitalism, even when they interpret texts unusually. They are readers, subject to a series of encouragements and discouragements in their ways of making meaning from the sources of information and entertainment that pass their way (Hartley 400). Those reading lives are quite chaotic as both interpretative moments and systems: for my informant Alec of Wallasey, Saturday nights in 1962 meant being allowed to stay up late to watch the series because his mother thought she looked like Honor Blackman. The show also served as Alec's introduction to unusual narrative form. For Margaret of Manhattan, TV was strictly rationed except when the babysitter was in charge, and *The Avengers* was on at just the right time of the week. For Tom of Rockhampton, 'the marvel of ju-jitsu and pretty women laying hunks of men low . . . gave us small people who were bullied in the school yard some hope'. Little wonder that Peter O'Toole confided 'only Mrs Gale . . . could induce him to leave the pubs before closing time'. For contemporary actresses, the series provided more emulation than distraction: Lucy Lawless, star of Sam Raimi's 1996 syndication success *Xena: Warrior Princess*, based her performance on Diana Rigg, while Gillian Anderson from *The X-Files* was a *New Avengers* fan (O'Toole, cited in Macnee and Cameron 228; Grimes; Swallow).

Some of these processes have an impact on producers, especially when in search of overseas sales. Clemens attributed the series' success outside Britain to representing the country 'not as it is, but as people think it is. . . . The Britishness was quite deliberate and very successful' (Clemens, quoted in Sutcliffe 30). That involves the quaintest of calculations: how to imagine and then image another country's imaginary of your own symbolic universe. Dennis Spooner, one of the writers, put it this way:

> We showed England as the world thinks it is, and England as England would like it to be. It's true. If you go to America, they think of London either as it's described by Charles Dickens or by *The Avengers*. It's the shorthand of this world. (Spooner, quoted in Auty)

There is a strange vein of superiority and inferiority running through the publicity stories produced for the American market, consisting in equal parts of a belief that the series represents the old world, a time and place superseded by the manifest modernity of the United States, and the counter-position that finds the USA somehow less than fully formed, with a self-doubting frown on the other side of its smirk at the UK. This differentiation from the norms of North American mythology may have made *The Avengers* available to a creative uptake by others marginalised from that freedom fantasy. Young African-Americans growing up in the 1960s lacked black heroes on prime time, although espionage was a breakthrough with *I Spy* and *Mission: Impossible*. Steed and Emma were reportedly admired by many such viewers, in the relative absence of people of colour. This may be because of the difficulty for anybody (other than some Surrey commuters) of identifying with Steed, given his ridiculous attire and behavioural absurdity. Steed is seductive while being quite 'other' to most of us, despite critiques that read the very series title as an 'invitation to identify' with conservative politics (Amory 14 May 1966; Copage; Peter Forster; Hope; Schlesinger, Murdock and Elliott 79).

Maybe women viewers saw sexually uninhibited female characters who dressed for power and knew how to exercise it over assailants, while men interpreted such physical efficiency as both a challenge and a promise (Keenan 73). My informant jbenn, who was growing up in the USA during reruns of the series, put it this way:

> I used to write JB (me) + PM (Steed) on the foggy windows of the school bus. Mrs Peel was my idol. I even took ju-jitsu lessons as well [as] fencing lessons. Mrs Peel was an underlying influence on my perception of what a woman could be; super-intelligent, strong, versatile, creative, dangerous, beautiful, etc., equal and better than equal to most men. [S]he is one of my heroes.

Despite Macnee's lack of sting by comparison with Rigg, he was a model instance of a man enjoying women's company and caring about them. To Alex, growing up in the Californian suburbs in the 1960s, this made for 'a chaste yet sexually satisfying relationship (achieved through banter and smiles)'. It was sex through discourse. To Florent of Lille and his friends, Steed's Britishness was the programme's defining quality. His gentlemanly demeanour was something to mock, but also to admire. The phlegm of the British, that hold of self-control, always evokes two reactions from its audience: contempt and envy. *The Avengers* engaged pure envy, because – as for Ian of Shepperton – Steed's normalcy was a reassuring anchor among the unreality of the villains.

The series still thrives on this kind of response. Home pages on the World Wide Web see followers post images, sounds and opinions about the series. James Dawe's address was visited 600 times in June 1995, its first month. Between then and mid-February 1996 there were 35,727 visits, expanding to 154,939 by August 1997.

Disclaimers had entered the story when textual property laws produced the formulation: 'Please be aware that neither I nor this page have any connection with The Avengers.' Strange, isn't it, that capitalism makes imaginary figures real? Pictures, mostly of Rigg in leather, could be expanded to fill the screen and downloaded. Favourites include both profile shots and a series of action tableaux that see villains tumbling to the floor. Some of these clearly engage the banal male gaze, for instance a pose of Mrs Peel with her hand between her legs in a way we associate with the early 90s Madonna; but others play with roles (Rigg in Macnee's clothes).

At the *Diabolical Masterminds and Extraordinary Agents* Web Site, visitors vote for their favourite series villain. Other new sites since 1996 are *The Avengers-Mit Schirm, Charme und Melone, No.3, Stable Mews*, a second *New Avengers* site, *Elan, The Avengers All Things Emma Peel, The Trials and Tribulations of Emma Peel*, and *The Avengers Universe* (for fan fiction) via the mysterious emmapeel@hotmail.com (J. Lane; Kucinski; De Long; Mathews and Pimentel-Pinto; Pickering). January 1997 saw a discussion group at alt.tv.avengers on Usenet.

Avengers weekends are held annually for keen followers. Participants book in at a St Albans hotel. From there, they venture out to the Three Horseshoes, a Letchmore Heath pub used in 'Man-Eater of Surrey Green' and 'Dead Man's Treasure'. After further location sightings, they settle down to a quiz night, a video session, and a thematic treasure-hunt. A 1995 field trip by the weekenders led to a colour photograph posted on the Web of dedicated enthusiasts aboard the miniature train used in 'The Gravediggers'. July 14, 1996 saw the tenth Annual Dead Man's Treasure Hunt by series fans. Such followers differentiate themselves from obsessed fans: they are connoisseurs, not mad people. A discrete distance is taken from Trekkies and their *USS Enterprise* outfits, just as the 1960s *Avengers* fanzines prided themselves on not 'indulging in the usual icky trivia and personality obsession' of their kind. Excursion organisers Anthony McKay and Annette McKay have published a guide to locations used for British TV drama series that is named after *The Avengers*. A mix of nostalgia and the modern is evident in their reading and riding instructions to tourists: 'Avengerland includes some of the South of England's most unspoilt and peaceful spots,'

so it is essential to 'drive carefully on the country lanes and watch out for horse riders'. The guide was 'compiled after years of detective work' so that we can 'drive down the same roads as *Steed and Mrs Peel*'. Each site is detailed by the episode and action that took place there, and although 25 different series are included, from the 1950s to the 1990s, it is clear where true affection lies. And the 1990s audience that learnt to love early episodes of the Blackman era, thanks to repertory seasons by Channel Four in Britain and

Before Madonna, before Michael Jackson

157

A&E in the USA, was full of admiration for the cheapness of the production values along with the stylish boldness of the demeanour. *Starburst* magazine recommended that readers purchase classic episodes on tape for Christmas 1995 by tracking backwards in order to cultivate an appreciation of early shows in the correct manner (Barber; Schultz 14; McKay and McKay 1, back cover; Auty; Berkmann; McIlhoney 47–8).

Looking back on the series in 1993, Rigg argued that Mrs Peel had been 'an icon for the feminist movement in America'; female fans continued to send letters about her role-model function in their youth (Rigg, quoted in Sweeting). This was a major appeal for my informants Paola of Vermicate and Sarah from Portland, Oregon. For Bev of Hobart the effect was much more to do with fantasy and improbability than emulation, while Houlihan-Skilton felt competitive with the female leads for Macnee's affections. The outcomes are identical in one sense: engaged spectatorship. The *Guardian*'s TV critic of the 1990s, Katie Puckrik, reminisced like this:

> I'd been too young to understand why I was digging it, I got off on the constant carnal question-mark that hung in the air. . . . All that stiff courtesy between a man in a steel-rimmed bowler and a woman in a plastic catsuit – someone crack a window!

It had been a 'national addiction' to 'ever unfulfilled sex' (Randall).

Macnee has acknowledged the superb timing of the series in terms of second-wave feminism, in a way that puts its success squarely in the hands of its audience:

> Women were leaving their homes, their kitchens and their crèches in droves and going out and starting to throw men over their shoulders, which they've been doing ever since. It was sheer luck that the women's movement was starting to get going then. It lifted the series right up. (Macnee, quoted in Porter 39)

How should we interpret this scene from 'Death of a Great

Dane'? Mrs Gale enters a room in her apartment. She is filmed from the waist down, putting some music on a record-player and kicking off her shoes. A man creeps up from behind and yanks his tie around her neck. She throws and then overpowers him; and the event is diegetically unmotivated and unexplained! Attempts to fix the meaning of this scene in conventional sexist terms or realist story forms are doubly undermined, by her successful retaliation and the lack of reason behind the segment. There is, then, a play here between deeply orthodox methods of sexual representation, new ideas about gender and power, generic norms and formal innovation. Like the Bond persona, this complex amalgam may be decoded by different audiences as sadistic snobbery, modern transcendence, libertine promise, amateurish dash, organisational obedience, new technological heroism and outmoded imperial folly. For Kingsley Amis, writing in mid-1960s Britain, Steed is the worthy inheritor of a tradition that puts the hero above ordinary people, 'right at the opposite end of the social scale from the wretched Inspector Barlow' of *Z Cars* (Denning 213; Amis 4). For Claudia growing up in Stade in the late 1970s, reruns on German television provided a literal model for dressing up her Barbie dolls as Mrs Peel. How that mix of political categories and childhood actions is made sense of will depend very much on the sewing- or tool-kits that viewers bring with them to the text.

And there was always something encouraging a wry interpretation. 'The Positive Negative Man' coda finds Steed magnetised to a car.

> *Mrs Peel:* What are you? AC or DC?
> *Steed:* I've never had occasion to find out.
> *Mrs Peel:* Here, I'll give you a hand. [She becomes stuck as well]
> *Steed:* Don't fight it, Mrs Peel. We're inseparable.

And so say all of us. With residual payments coming in to the principals from reruns, and Emma's punctuation-mark still dangling, both they *and* their followers can afford to smile, certain that we know what we mean when we say 'I love *The Avengers*.'

Note on informants

To enrich this study with the observations and experiences of other viewers, I corresponded and spoke with a number of fans and television historians/theorists (these categories frequently over-lapped). My method in this was threefold. I was kindly given space on James Dawe's *Avengers* web page to mention my research and invite visitors to contact me with opinions and reminiscences. Many did so. Secondly, I emailed people I knew or knew of who may have views. Thirdly, I asked the graduate students in my Department for their recollections. The upshot of this was that I had informants from Canada, England, Italy, Wales, France, Germany, five states of Australia, and eight states of the US. The questions I asked were: What do you remember of the program? What were the physical circumstances of watching it – when did the program air, where were you, how old, and with whom? When you look back on *The Avengers*, what it does it mean to you?

Bibliography

Advertisement. *Variety*, 26 March 1969, p. 75.

Afton, Richard, 'Boring' *Evening News*, 28 October 1976, n. p.

— 'It's a Load of Tripe, Corn – and Yorkshire Pudding', *Evening News*, 20 October 1977, n. p.

— 'Schoolboy Stuff', *Evening News*, 15 September 1977, n. p.

'The All-Star, All-Time TV Hall of Fame', *Vanity Fair*, no. 424, December 1995, pp. 225–65, 290–1.

Alsop, Neil, 'Leather to Lacy', *Primetime*, no. 9, winter 1984–5, pp 16–19.

alt.t.avengers.

Amis, Kingsley, *The James Bond Dossier* (New York: New American Library, 1965).

Amory, Cleveland, 'Review', *TV Guide*, vol. 14, no. 20, 14 May 1966, p. 1.

— 'Review', *TV Guide*, vol. 15, no. 17, 29 April 1967, p. 27.

— 'Review', *TV Guide*, vol. 21, no. 43, 27 October 1973, p. 32.

Andrae, Thomas, 'Television's First Feminist: *The Avengers* and Female Spectatorship', *Discourse*, vol. 18, no. 3, spring 1996, pp. 112–36.

Arras, Jean, 'Diana: She Glitters', *TV Guide*, vol. 21, no. 39, 29 September 1973, pp. 38–40.

Auty, Chris, 'Who Made "The Avengers"', *Sunday Times*, 31 October 1982, p. 62.

'The Avenger Tries on a TV Role . . . Not to Mention a Skimpy Dress', *TV Guide*, vol. 21, no. 7, 17 February 1973, pp. 12–13.

'The Avengers', *Variety*, 25 September 1968, n. p.

'"The Avengers" Change Gear for a New Series' press release, n. d.

'Avengers Go East', *Evening Standard*, 15 March 1968, n. p.

The Avengers. Episodes referred to and approximate dates of first UK transmission (sources vary on this information): 'The Bird Who Knew Too Much' 11-2-67; 'Bizarre' 14-9-69; 'Castle De'ath'

30-10-65; 'The Charmers' 29-2-64; 'The Cybernauts' 14-10-65; 'The Danger Makers' 12-2-66; 'Dead Men's Treasure' 21-10-67; 'Death at Bargain Prices' 21-10-65; 'Death of a Batman' 26-10-63; 'Death of a Great Dane' 17-11-62; 'Dial a Deadly Number' 4-12-65; 'Don't Look Behind You' 14-12-63; 'Epic' 1-4-67; 'Escape in Time' 28-1-67; 'Fog' 23-6-69; 'The Forget-Me-Knot' 12-1-69; 'The Frighteners' 27-5-61; 'From Venus with Love' 13-1-67; 'Game' 2-10-68; 'The Gilded Cage' 9-11-63; 'The Girl From A.U.N.T.I.E.' 21-1-66; 'The Gravediggers' 7-10-65; 'The Hidden Tiger' 4-3-67; 'The Hour That Never Was' 27-11-65; 'The House That Jack Built' 5-3-66; 'Immortal Clay' 13-1-63; 'The Joker' 29-4-67; 'Legacy of Death' 9-3-69; 'The Little Wonders' 11-1-64; 'The Living Dead' 25-2-67; 'Look (Stop Me If You've Heard This One) But There Were These Two Fellers' 4-12-68; 'Mandrake' 25-1-64; 'The Man-Eater of Surrey Green' 11-12-65; 'The Master Minds' 6-11-65; 'Mission . . . Highly Inprobable' 18-11-67; 'The Morning After' 11-5-69; 'Murdersville' 11-11-67; 'November Five' 2-11-63; 'The Nutshell' 19-10-63; 'The Positive Negative Man' 4-11-67; 'Return of the Cybernauts' 30-9-67; 'Second Sight' 16-11-63; 'The Secrets Broker' 1-2-64; 'The See-Through Man' 4-2-67; 'Silent Dust' 1-1-66; 'Small Game for Big Hunters' 14-1-66; 'The Superlative Seven' 8-4-67; 'A Surfeit of H_2O' 20-11-65; 'They Keep Killing Steed' 6-4-69; 'Thingumajig' 2-4-69; 'Too Many Christmas Trees' 23-12-65; 'A Touch of Brimstone' 18-2-66; 'The Town of No Return' 2-10-65; 'The Undertakers' 5-10-63; and 'The Winged Avenger' 18-2-67.

The Avengers Universe. http://members.tripod.com/~Phoenixxx/index.html

Bacon-Smith, Camille, *Enterprising Women: Television Fandom and the Creation of Popular Myth* (Philadelphia: University of Pennsylvania Press, 1992).

Bakewell, Joan, 'Twenty Years On', *The Listener*, vol. 96, no. 2486, 2 December 1976, pp. 723–4.

Banks-Smith, Nancy, 'The Avengers', *Guardian*, 21 October 1976, n. p.

— 'Cathy's Gone – And So Have the Gasps', *Sun*, 29 September 1965, n. p.

—— 'Dash of Batman, Touch of the Thunderbirds', *Sun*, 29 September 1967, n. p.

—— *Sun*, 26 September 1968, n. p.

Barber, George, 'Hell for Leather', *Independent Magazine*, 13 August 1994, pp. 42–4.

Barnouw, Erik, *Tube of Plenty: The Evolution of American Television*, rev. ed. (Oxford: Oxford University Press, 1982).

Bassom, David, 'Linda Thorson', *Starburst*, special no. 20, July 1994, pp. 64–7.

Beale, Lewis, 'Back with Avengeance', *Daily News*, 19 October 1995, p. 57.

Berkmann, Marcus, *Daily Mail*, 5 February 1993, p. 40.

Bianculli, David, 'Sexy "Avengers"', *New York Post*, 23 January 1991, p. 72.

—— *Dictionary of Teleliteracy: Television's 500 Biggest Hits, Misses, and Events* (New York: Continuum, 1996).

'Biba Leathers', *Skin Two*, no. 13, 1993, p. 17.

Biederman, Danny, '*The Avengers*' Patrick Macnee: Cool Before it was Hip', *Emmy*, vol. 13, no. 2, April 1991, pp. 26–9.

Billington, Michael, 'Time for a Rest', *Times*, 4 March 1969, n. p.

Black, Peter, *Sunday Times*, 23 March 1966, n. p.

—— 'Undercover and Out of Mind, Except for that Mrs Gale', *Daily Mail*, 13 October 1962, n. p.

Blyth, Alan, 'ITV: The Avengers', *Daily Express*, 8 October 1965, n. p.

Booker, Christopher, *The Neophiliacs: A Study of the Revolution in English Life in the Fifties and Sixties* (London: Collins, 1969).

Briggs, Asa, *Competition: The History of Broadcasting in the United Kingdom, Volume V* (Oxford: Oxford University Press, 1995).

Brooks, Tim and Earle Marsh, *The Complete Directory to Prime Time Network TV Shows 1946–Present*, 3rd edn (New York: Ballentine Books, 1985).

Brown, Richard and Diana Rigg, 'Dialogue with Diana', *Today's Film Maker*, vol. 1, no. 4, 1972, pp. 21, 53–6.

Brunsdon, Charlotte, 'Problems with Quality', *Screen*, vol. 31, no. 1, 1990, pp. 67–90.

Burchill, Julie, *Girls on Film* (New York: Pantheon Books, 1986).

Buxton, David, *From 'The Avengers' to 'Miami Vice': Form and Ideology in Television Series* (Manchester: Manchester University Press, 1990).

Canby, Vincent, 'T.V.: "Avengers" is Unveiled by A.B.C.: Another Secret Agent Arrives on Scene', *New York Times*, 29 March 1966, p. 8B.

Carlton, John, 'Pussy Galore', *Man*, vol. 58, no. 2, July 1965, pp. 32–4.

Carrazé, Alain and Jean-Luc Putheaud, *Chapeau Melon et Bottes de Cuir* (Paris: Huitième Art, 1990).

Carthew, Anthony, 'Tweedy Thriller', *New York Times*, 15 December 1963, p. X25.

Casa-Zza, Christophe, 'Emma, Tara, les Autres et Moi', in Alain Carrazé and Jean-Luc Putheaud, *Chapeau, Melon et Bottes de Cuir* (Paris: Huitième Art, 1990), p. 30.

Chartier, Roger, 'Texts, Printings, Readings', in Lynn Hunt (ed.), *The New Cultural History* (Berkeley: University of California Press, 1989), pp. 154–75.

Chibnall, Steve, 'Avenging the Past'. *New Society*, 28 March 1985, p. 476.

Clarke, John, 'Enter the Cybernauts: Problems in postmodernism', *Communication*, vol. 10, nos. 3–4, 1988, pp. 383–401.

Clayton, Sylvia, *Sunday Telegraph*, 20 October 1976, n. p.

Collins, Richard, *Culture, Communication, and National Identity: The Case of Canadian Television* (Toronto: University of Toronto Press, 1990).

Cook, Richard, 'A Thoroughly British Affair', *New Musical Express*, 20 November 1982, p. 6.

Cooper, R. W., 'Birds at Centre of Espionage', *Times*, 11 February 1967, n. p.

Copage, Eric, 'About Men; Prime-Time Heroes', *New York Times*, 2 February 1992, Section 6 Magazine Desk, p. 12.

Coren, Alan, 'The New Avengers', *Times*, 17 November 1976, n. p.

Cornell, Paul, Martin Day and Keith Topping, *The Guinness Book of Classic British TV* (Enfield: Guinness Publishing, 1993).

The Avengers Programme Guide (London: Virgin, 1994).

Cosgrove, Vincent, 'Mrs Peel, How Nice to Have You Back', *Daily News*, 24 March 1987, pp. 8–9.

Craig, Patricia and Mary Cadogan, *The Lady Investigates: Women Detectives and Spies in Fiction* (New York: St Martin's Press, 1981).

'Crib Sheet', *Mail on Sunday*, 24 October 1993, p. 80.

Critchley, Julian, 'Avengers Still Good with Miss Thorson'. *Times*, 10 October 1968, n. p.

Cullis, Kevin, 'Television', *Tribune*, 29 October 1976, n. p.

Cummings, Jen, *Jen Cummings' Avengers Home Page*. http://www.gla.ac.uk/Clubs/WebSoc/~9504977c/avengers-index.html

Curthoys, Ann and John Docker, 'In Praise of *Prisoner*', in John Tulloch and Graeme Turner (eds), *Australian Television: Programmes, Pleasures and Politics* (Sydney: Allen and Unwin, 1989), pp. 52–71.

Danto, Arthur C., *Beyond the Brillo Box: The Visual Arts in Post-Historical Perspective* (New York: Noonday Press, 1992).

Davies, Tristan, 'Why Steed Never Got to Play Hamlet', *Guardian*, 1993, n. p.

Davis, Fred, *Fashion, Culture, and Identity* (Chicago: University of Chicago Press, 1992).

Davis, Hank, 'Relationship', *En Garde*, no. 6, 1969, pp. 79–82.

Dawe, James, *James Dawe's Avengers Home Page*. http://nyquist.ee.ualberta.ca/~dawe/avengers.html

Dean, Peter, 'Wind Up', *Sight and Sound*, vol. 3, no. 11, November 1993, p. 62.

DeAndrea, William L., *Encyclopedia Mysteriosa: A Comprehensive Guide to the Art of Detection in Print, Film, Radio, and Television* (New York: Prentice Hall, 1994).

de Blasio, Ed, 'Thanks Yanks', *Photoplay*, April 1968, pp. 34–5, 70, 82.

de Bono, John, 'Vengeance for The Avengers', *Weekend Telegraph*, 15 February 1992, p. 27.

Déja Vu advertisement, *Hollywood Collectables*, vol. 1, no. 9, September 1994, pp. 2–3, 67.

De Long, Heather, No.3, *Stable Mews*. http://www.mindspring.com/~dscully/torihtml

Denning, Michael, 'Licensed to Look: James Bond and the Heroism of Consumption', in Francis Mulhern (ed.), *Contemporary Marxist Literary Criticism* (London: Longman, 1992), pp. 211–29.

'Diana Rigg and the Emmapeeler', *TV Guide*, June 1967, n. p.

Dishwalla, 'Miss Emma Peel', on *Pet Your Friends*. Written by Scott Alexander, Rodney Browning, J. R. Richards and George Prendergast. A & M Records, 1995.

Donaldson, Marie, '"The Gilded Cage"' press release. ABC Weekend 4 November 1963.

— '"The Little Wonders"' press release. ABC Weekend 6 January 1964.

— 'Steed Fights a Battle of the Mind' press release. ABC Television October 1965.

— 'They've Got Their Own Fur to Keep Them Warm' press release. ABC Television October 1965.

— 'Transmission Schedule Up to Christmas' press release. ABC Television Autumn 1965.

'Dressed to Kill', *Buying Satellite*, February 1994, pp. 44–7.

Dunkley, Chris, 'The New Avengers', *Financial Times*, 20 October 1976, n. p.

Dunn, Peter, *Sunday Times*, 11 September 1977, n. p.

Durgnat, Raymond, *A Mirror for England: British Movies from Austerity to Affluence* (London: Faber and Faber, 1970).

East, Andy, *The Cold War File* (Metuchen: Scarecrow Press, 1983).

Eco, Umberto, 'A Correspondence with Umberto Eco: Genova-Bologna-Binghamton-Bloomington August–September, 1982 March–April, 1983', trans. Carolyn Springer, *boundary* 2, vol. 12, no. 1, 1983, pp. 1–13.

— *Travels in Hyperreality: Essays*, trans. William Weaver (London: Picador, 1987).

Eder, Bruce, 'A License to Thrill', *Village Voice*, 5 February 1991, n. p.

'An Edwardian in Malibu: The Ultra-British Patrick Macnee Prefers California's Beaches to London's Drawing Rooms', *TV Guide*, vol. 16, no. 46, 16 November 1968, pp. 18–20.

Efron, Edith, 'Is Television Making a Mockery of the American Woman?', *TV Guide*, vol. 18, no. 32, 8 August 1970, pp. 6–9.

'Em Appeal', *British Vogue*, August 1990, n. p.

En Garde, no. 6, 1969.

'The Entertainers 7: Nicole Kidman', *Entertainment Weekly*, nos. 307–8, 29 December 1995–5 January 1996, pp. 34–5.

'Entretien avec Diane Rigg', trans. Bruno Billion, in Alain Carrazé and Jean-Luc Putheaud, *Chapeau, Melon et Bottes de Cuir* (Paris:

Huitième Art, 1990), p. 16.

Erickson, Hal, *Syndicated Television: The First Forty Years, 1947–1987* (Jefferson: McFarland and Company, 1989).

Eveling, Stanley, *Scotsman*, 22 October 1983, p. 3.

Fakrikian, David, 'Chapeau, Melon et Bottes de Cuir: Objets de Culte', *Géneration de Séries*, no. 13, spring 1995, pp. 38–41.

— 'Les Projets de Films "Avengers": Mission Très Improbable', *Géneration de Séries*, no. 12, winter 1995, pp. 18–20.

Fiddy, Dick, 'Dog and Cat', *Primetime*, no. 9, winter 1984–5, pp. 20–1.

— 'In Surrey Green a Plant is Eating People . . . !?', *Primetime*, vol. 1, no. 1, 1981, p. 13.

Forster, P., *Spectator*, 24 March 1961, n. p.

Forster, Peter, 'Steed Minus Style', *Evening Standard*, 20 October 1976, n. p.

'French Finance Return of "The Avengers"', *Times*, 8 December 1975, n. p.

Frensham, Ray, 'How Clemens' Professional Ambition Paid Off', *Television Today*, 2 July 1992, n. p.

Frith, Simon, 'The Good, the Bad, and the Indifferent: Defending Popular Culture from the Populists', *Diacritics*, vol. 21, no. 4, 1991, pp. 102–15.

Fulton, Roger, *The Encyclopedia of TV Science Fiction* (n. pl.: Boxtree, 1990).

Furlong, Monica, *Daily Mail*, 15 October 1965, n. p.

Gabriel, Trip, 'Wicked Fashion Sitcom? Delicious! Pity it's Fiction', *New York Times*, 10 July 1994, Section 1 Style Desk, p. 31.

Gambaccini, Paul and Rod Taylor, *Television's Greatest Hits: Every Hit Television Programme Since 1960* (London: Network Books, 1993).

Gamman, Lorraine, 'Watching the Detectives: The Enigma of the Female Gaze', in Lorraine Gamman and Margaret Marshment (eds), *The Female Gaze: Women as Viewers of Popular Culture* (Seattle: The Real Comet Press, 1989), pp. 8–26.

Gamson, Joshua, *Claims to Fame: Celebrity in Contemporary America* (Berkeley: University of California Press, 1994).

Garforth, John, *The Passing of Gloria Munday* (London: Panther Books, 1967).

Gent, Paul, 'Catsuit Capers', *Listener*, vol. 114, no. 2918, 18 July 1985, pp. 31–2.

Gianakos, Larry James, *Television Drama Programming: A Comprehensive Chronicle, 1959–1975* (Metuchen: Scarecrow Press, 1978).

Giles, Dennis, 'A Structural Analysis of the Police Story', in Stuart M. Kaminsky with Jeffrey H. Mahan, *American Television Genres* (Chicago: Nelson-Hall, 1985), pp. 67–84.

Ginsburg, Mark, 'Mrs Peel's Wheels', *Vanity Fair*, vol. 54, no. 3, March 1991, pp. 192–4.

Goldberg, Lee, *Unsold Television Pilots 1955 through 1988* (Jefferson: McFarland and Company, 1990).

'Good-Chap Sexuality', *Newsweek*, 4 April 1966, p. 84.

Gowers, Michael, 'First Kiss', *Daily Mail*, 6 January 1964, n. p.

Grant, Linda, 'Valley Girls', *Radio Times*, vol. 261, no. 3411, 22–8 April 1989, p. 13.

Green, Timothy, *The Universal Eye: World Television in the Seventies* (London: The Bodley Head, 1972).

Greenberg, Cara, 'Want the 90's to Fade Away? Try Retro-Life', *New York Times*, 30 April 1992, Section C Home Desk, p. 1.

Grimes, Williams, 'A Woman Wielding Many Weapons, Among Them a Sneer and a Stare', *New York Times Television*, 19–25 May 1996, Section 12, pp. 4–5, 18, 22.

Gross, Ben, 'Singers Fill Music Hall: "The Avengers" Return', *Daily News*, 11 January 1968, n. p.

Haining, Peter, ed., *The Television Crimebusters Omnibus: Great Stories of the Police Detectives* (London: Orion, 1994).

Hamermesh, Daniel S. and Jeff E. Biddle, 'Beauty and the Labor Market', *American Economic Review*, vol. 84, no. 5, 1994, pp. 1174–94.

Hano, Arnold, 'Tall Redheads Always Get Caught', *TV Guide*, vol. 21, no. 40, 6 October 1973, pp. 30–9.

Harrington, C. Lee and Denise D. Bielby, *Soap Fans: Pursuing Pleasure and Making Meaning in Everyday Life* (Philadelphia: Temple University Press, 1995).

Hartley, John, 'Twoccing and Joyreading', *Textual Practice*, vol. 8, no. 3, 1994, pp. 399–413.

Haug, W. F., *Critique of Commodity Aesthetics: Appearance,*

Sexuality and Advertising in Capitalist Society, trans. Robert
Bock (Cambridge: Polity Press, 1986).

Himmelweit, Hilde T, Betty Swift and Marianne E. Jaeger, 'The
Audience as Critic: A Conceptual Analysis of Entertainment',
in Percy H. Tannenbaum (ed.), *The Entertainment Functions of
Television* (Hillsdale: Lawrence Erlbaum, 1980), pp. 67–106.

Hirshorn, Louis, 'Patrick Macnee', *TV Zone*, no. 16, n. d., pp. 16–19.

Hochswender, Woody, 'Patterns', *New York Times*, 1 May 1990,
Section B Style Desk, p. 7.

Hodgson, Pamela, 'The Liberated Avenger: She Packs All the Punch
of an Emma Peel, But Has a Mind of Her Own', *Daily Mail*, 21
January 1985, p. 1.

Hope, Francis, 'Thriller Plus', *New Statesman*, 31 January 1964,
n. p.

Houldsworth, Richard, 'The Cybernauts', *TV Zone*, no. 67, n. d.,
pp. 35–7.

Houlihan-Skilton, Mary, 'Slick "Avengers" Series is Making Cable
Comeback', *Chicago Sun-Times*, 9 November 1990, Weekend
Plus, p. 3.

Howarth, Steve and Chris Lyons, 'The Belles of St Clemens',
Dreamwatch, vol. 2, no. 9, May 1996, pp. 35–7.

Howkins, John, *Understanding Television: The Story of TV Past,
Present and Future* (London: Sundial Books, 1976).

Hume, Alan, 'Filming for Colour Television Series', *British
Kinematography Sound and Television*, vol. 50, no. 1, January
1968, pp. 4–10.

Hunter, Ian, 'Providence and Profit: Speculations in the Genre
Market', *Southern Review*, vol. 22, no. 3, 1988, pp. 211–23.

Ironside, Virginia, 'TV', *Sunday Mail*, 5 December 1968, n. p.

Jackson, Martin, 'Steed's New Girl – Linda Thorson', *Daily Express*,
26 September 1968, n. p.

James, Clive, 'The New Avengers', *Observer*, 7 November 1976, n. p.

Jenkins, Henry, *Textual Poachers: Television Fans and Participatory
Culture* (New York: Routledge, 1992).

Johnson, Kirk, 'At Work and Play With: Dr Oliver Sacks; Looking
Inward, Understanding Strange Worlds', *New York Times*,
23 October 1996, Section C Living Desk p. 1.

Kaminsky, Stuart M. with Jeffrey H. Mahan, *American Television*

Genres (Chicago: Nelson-Hall, 1985).

Keenan, Brigid, *The Women We Wanted to Look Like* (New York: St Martin's Press, 1977).

Kelly, Jane, 'Vengeance is Mine: Patrick Macnee is Back, and This Time He's in it for the Money', *Daily Mail*, 28 October 1993, p. 9.

Kerr, Paul, 'Watching the Detectives', *Primetime*, vol. 1, no. 1, 1981, pp. 2–6.

Knowles, Stewart, 'TV World', *TV Times*, 26 January–1 February 1985, p. 23.

Koldys, Mark, 'Diana Rigg', *Films in Review*, vol. 21, no. 3, 1970, p. 192.

Kozloff, Sarah, 'Narrative Theory and Television', in Robert C. Allen (ed.), *Channels of Discourse, Reassembled: Television and Contemporary Criticism*, 2nd edn (Chapel Hill: University of North Carolina Press, 1992), pp. 67–100.

Kretzner and Lee, 'Kinky Boots', pub. Essex Music.

Kucinski, Stefan, *The Avengers-Mit Schirm, Charme und Melone.* http://ourworld.compuserve.com/homepages/Kucinski/ stku_av.htm

La Ferla, Ruth, 'Fashion: If the Suit Fits . . . Wear It', *New York Times*, 2 September 1990, Section 6 Magazine, p. 41.

— 'Fashion: Take the Plunge', *New York Times*, 10 February 1991, Section 6 Magazine Desk, p. 51.

Laing, Stuart, 'Banging in Some Reality: The Original "Z Cars"', in John Corner (ed.), *Popular Television in Britain: Studies in Cultural History* (London: BFI, 1991), pp. 125–44.

Landy, Marcia, *British Genres: Cinema and Society, 1930–1960* (Princeton: Princeton University Press, 1991).

Lane, Jackie, *Diabolical Masterminds and Extraordinary Agents.* http://www.mindspring.com/~jglane/avenger.htm

Lane, Stewart, 'Million Dollars for What?', *Daily Worker*, 27 November 1965, n. p.

Laumer, Keith, *The Avengers #7: 'The Gold Bomb'* (New York: Berkley Medallion, 1968).

le Carré, John, 'Spying ... the Passion of My Time', *Queen's Quarterly*, vol. 100, no. 2, summer 1993, pp. 269–72.

Leets, Laura, Gavin de Becker and Howard Giles, 'Fans: Exploring

Expressed Motivations for Contacting Celebrities', *Journal of Language and Social Psychology*, vol. 14, nos. 1–2, 1995, pp. 102–23.

Lewis, Jon E. and Penny Stempel, *Cult TV: The Essential Critical Guide* (London: Pavilion Books, 1993).

Lewis, Lisa A., 'Introduction', in Lisa A. Lewis (ed.), *The Adoring Audience: Fan Culture and Popular Media* (London: Routledge, 1992), pp. 1–6.

Lockwood, Lyn, 'Dressed to Style in New "Avengers" ', *Daily Telegraph*, 29 September 1965, n. p.

Lowry, Maxine, 'They get Color Next Year, but we get Macnee Now', *New York World-Telegram*, 21 March 1966, p. 10.

Lunenfeld, Peter, 'GenreAlizations: Genre Theory in Film Studios', *Spectator*, vol. 12, no. 2, 1992, pp. 6–15.

Lurie, Alison, *The Language of Clothes* (New York: Random House, 1981).

MacDonald, J. Fred, *Television and the Red Menace: The Video Road to Vietnam* (New York: Praeger, 1985).

McGowan, Alastair, *Elan*. http://www.mech.gla.ac.uk/~alistair/bowler/avenge.htm

McIlhoney, Lawrence, 'Videofile', *Starburst*, vol. 18, no. 4, December 1995, pp. 46–8.

McKay, Anthony and Annette McKay, *A Guide to Avengerland: A Listing of Over 250 Locations used in the Filming of Class British Television Series* (Doncaster: Time Screen, 1993).

McKay, Anthony and Michael Richardson, 'The Avengers Man: An Interview with Brian Clemens', *Time Screen*, no. 19, autumn 1992, pp. 21–33.

Macnee, Patrick, 'Foreword', in John Peel and Dave Rogers, *The Avengers: Too Many Targets* (New York: St Martin's Press, 1990), n. p.

— 'Trente Ans Après', trans. Bruno Billion, in Alain Carrazé and Jean-Luc Putheaud, *Chapeau Melon et Bottes de Cuir* (Paris: Huitième Art, 1990), pp. 13–14.

— and Marie Cameron, *Blind in One Ear: The Avengers Returns* (San Francisco: Mercury House, 1989).

Macpherson, Don, 'Delightful Decadence', *Sunday Times Magazine*, 13 March 1983, n. p.

Malitz, Nancy, 'Invasion of the Girls Surprises Video-Game Makers', *New York Times*, 21 December 1995, p. C2.

Malone, M., *Daily Mirror*, 23 January 1969, n. p.

Mansell, John, 'Laurie Johnson', *Soundtrack!*, vol. 14, no. 56, December 1995, pp. 28–30.

Mansfield, John, 'What a Way to Take a Trip', *En Garde*, no. 6, 1969, pp. 22–8.

Marsland, L., 'Mrs Gale Will Claim the Throne', *Daily Telegraph*, 9 March 1964, n. p.

Marton, Andrew, 'Film: Vintage TV Gets Replayed for Film', *New York Times*, 1 November 1992, Section 2 Arts and Leisure Desk, p. 30.

Mason, Francis, 'Nostalgia for the Future: The End of History and Postmodern "Pop" TV', *Journal of Popular Culture*, vol. 29, no. 4, spring 1996, pp. 27–40.

Matthews, Dave and James Pimentel-Pinto, http://www.personal. u-net.com/~carnfort/New Avengers/intro

M. Beat, 'Surrender', on *Jungle Hits Vol. 1*. Street Tuff Records, 1994.

'Meet Steed's Boss . . .' press release, n. d.

Melly, George, *Observer*, 29 September 1968, n. p.

— *Revolt into Style: The Pop Arts in Britain* (Harmondsworth: Penguin, 1972).

Menkes, Suzy, 'Runways: Scorned No Longer, Synthetics Go Modern', *New York Times*, 1 January 1995, Section 1 Style Desk, p. 41.

— 'In the World of Fashion, Leather is Indestructible', *New York Times*, 22 September 1996, Style Desk pp. 49, 52.

Merlman, Richard M., 'Power and Community in Television', in Horace Newcomb (ed.), *Television: The Critical View* (New York: Oxford University Press, 1976), pp. 86–104.

Meyers, Richard, *TV Detectives* (San Diego: AS Barnes; London: Tantivy Press, 1981).

Miller, Aileen, 'The Agonizing Choice Diana Rigg is Forced to Make: Her Husband or Her Career', *Silver Screen*, April 1974, pp. 60–1.

Morley, Sheridan, 'One into Three Will Go', *Radio Times*, vol. 214, no. 2782, 5 March 1977, pp. 66–9.

Morrison, Grant, 'Un Monde de Miraculeuses Métamorphoses', trans. David Fakrikian and Bruno Billion, in Alain Carrazé and

Jean-Luc Putheaud, *Chapeau, Melon et Bottes de Cuir* (Paris: Huitième Art, 1990), pp. 21–2.

Murdock, Graham, 'Televisual Tourism: National Image-Making and International Markets', in Christian W. Thomsen (ed.), *Cultural Transfer or Electronic Imperialism? The Impact of American Television Programs on European Television* (Heidelberg: Carl Winter Universitätsverlag, 1989), pp. 171–83.

Murray, James, 'Back with a Vengeance', *Daily Express*, 20 October 1976, n. p.

Musel, Robert, 'Can She Make Them Forget Mrs Peel?', *TV Guide*, vol. 16, no. 9, 2 March 1968, pp. 12–15.

— 'En Garde: Britain's Diana Rigg is Again After the American Viewer', *TV Guide*, vol. 15, no. 3, 21 January 1967, pp. 19–22.

— 'She's Miss Rigg of St John's Wood, Now', *TV Guide*, vol. 16, no. 31, 3 August 1968, pp. 16–18.

— 'Violence Can be Fun: In Britain, Everybody Laughs at "The Avengers" – Except the Audience', *TV Guide*, vol. 12, no. 19, 9 May 1964, pp. 12–14.

Nelson, Paul B., 'Cardinal Cardin: Pragmatic Prophet of the Pace-Setter', *Man*, vol. 62, no. 1, June 1967, pp. 78–80.

The New Avengers. Episodes referred to and approximate dates of first UK transmission: 'The Eagle's Nest' 19-10-76; 'Faces' 14-12-76; 'The Gladiators' 24-11-77; 'K is for Kill' (Parts I and II) 27-10-77 and 3-11-77; and 'The Last of the Cybernauts . . . ??' 2-11-76.

The New Avengers Home Page. http://www.ee.surrey.ac.uk/-Contrib/Entertainment/New Avengers/index.html

Nichols, Peter, 'Television; Ultimate Rerun', *New York Times*, 28 July 1991, Section 2 Arts and Leisure Desk, p. 25.

'Nico Icon', *New Yorker*, vol. 71, no. 46, 29 January 1996, p. 25.

Nolan, Jack Edmund, 'Films on TV', *Films in Review*, vol. 25, no. 8, October 1974, pp. 489–93.

O'Quinn, Kerry, 'The Avengers', liner notes to *The Avengers* suite CD, Varèse Sarabande Records, originally released 1980.

Owens, Mitchell, 'Design Notebook; In Search of a Pulse at High Point', *New York Times*, 4 May 1995, Section C Home Desk, p. 1.

Paglia, Camille, *Sexual Personae: Art and Decadence from Nefertiti to Emily Dickinson* (London: Yale University Press, 1990).

Papazian, Ed, *Medium Rare: The Evolution, Workings and Impact of Commercial Television* (New York: Medium Dynamics, 1989).

Paton, Maureen, *Daily Express*, 7 November 1984, p. 23.

Patrick, Tony, 'Present Tense? Let's Do the Time Warp Again', *Times*, 4 February 1995, p. 2.

Peel, John and Dave Rogers, *The Avengers: Too Many Targets* (New York: St Martin's Press, 1990).

'Peter Graham Scott: Classic Director', *TV Zone*, no. 62, n. d, pp. 24–5.

Pickering, Laura, *The Avengers All Things Emma Peel*. http://www.stayfree.co.uk/dialin/viper/

Porter, John, 'The Avengers', *Starburst*, vol. 16, no. 6, February 1994, pp. 38–42.

'Pre-Sales Put "New Avengers"' in the Black', *Variety*, 21 April 1976, n. p.

'Profile on . . . Patrick Macnee: John Steed in "The Avengers"'. press release, n. d.

Pronay, Nicholas, 'Sorry But It Seems to Have Been Junked', *Primetime*, vol. 1, no. 4, 1982, pp. 4–5.

Puckrik, Katie, 'The New Avengers', *Guardian*, 11 March 1995, p. 80.

Purser, Philip, *Sunday Telegraph*, 27 March 1966, n. p.

— *Sunday Telegraph*, 15 January 1967, n. p.

— 'Thoughtless Thriller', *Sunday Telegraph*, 3 October 1965, n. p.

Putheaud, Jean-Luc, 'Les Vengeurs Fantastiques', *Génération Séries*, no. 12, winter 1995, pp. 12–14.

Rand, Ayn, *The Romantic Manifesto: A Philosophy of Literature*, rev. edn (New York: Signet, 1975).

Randall, Neville, 'Long Live This King', *Daily Sketch*, 26 September 1968, n. p.

Raynor, Harry, 'No Offence in the World', *Times*, 28 September 1968, n. p.

Reynolds, Stanley, 'Weekend Television', *Guardian*, 16 January 1967, n. p.

Rhodes, Kate, 'Have *Cagney and Lacey* Cracked the Case? TV's Female Crime Fighters', *Metro*, no. 78, summer 1988–9, pp. 23–5.

Richardson, Maurice, *Observer*, 3 October 1965, n. p.

— 'On the Run', *Observer*, 7 November 1965, n. p.

Richardson, Michael, 'Under the Influence of The Avengers [Part 1]', *Primetime*, no. 15, 1989, pp. 7–13.

— 'Under the Influence of The Avengers [Part 2]', *Primetime*, no. 16, winter 1990–1, pp. 28–33.

Rivière, François, 'Une Conjuration de l'Élegance', in Alain Carrazé and Jean-Luc Putheaud, *Chapeau Melon et Bottes de Cuir* (Paris: Huitième Art, 1990), pp. 32–4.

Robinson, Nigel, 'The Avengers', *TV Zone*, special no. 4, n. d, pp. 37–40.

Rogers, Dave, *The Complete Avengers: Everything You Ever Wanted to Know About The Avengers and The New Avengers* (New York: St Martin's Press, 1989).

— *The ITV Encyclopedia of Adventure* (n. pl.: Boxtree, 1988).

Rose, Cynthia, 'Kinky', *New Musical Express*, 23 April 1983, p. 12.

Rosenthal, Sharon, 'From Karate Chops to Shakespeare', *TV Guide*, vol. 32, no. 3, 21 January 1984, pp. 10–12.

Rouse, Elizabeth, *Understanding Fashion* (Oxford: Blackwell Scientific Publications, 1989).

Rutherford, Paul, *When Television Was Young: Primetime Canada 1952–1967* (Toronto: University of Toronto Press, 1990).

Rutsky, R. L., 'Visible Sins, Vicarious Pleasures: Style and Vice in *Miami Vice*', *SubStance*, vol. 17, no. 1, 1988, pp. 77–82.

Salisbury, Lesley, 'You Can't Keep a Good Man Down', *TV Times*, vol. 109, no. 46, 13–19 November 1982, pp. 83–4.

Schiro, Anne-Marie, 'Review/Fashion; Hollywood on a Runway', *New York Times*, 7 March 1995, Section B Style Desk, p. 8.

— 'Review/Fashion; Smiles with Style: Lars and Johnson', *New York Times*, 2 November 1993, Section B Style Desk, p. 11.

Schlesinger, Philip, Graham Murdock and Philip Elliott, *Television 'Terrorism': Political Violence in Popular Culture* (London: Comedia, 1983).

Schrøder, Kim Christian, 'Cultural Quality: Search for a Phantom? A Reception Perspective on Judgements of Cultural Value', in Michael Skovmand and Kim Christian Schrøder (eds), *Media Cultures: Reappraising Transnational Media* (London: Routledge, 1992), pp. 199–219.

Schultz, Richard, 'Tacking', *En Garde*, no. 6, 1969, pp. 4–19.

Sendall, Bernard, *Independent Television in Britain vol. 1: Origin and Foundation, 1946–62* (London: Macmillan, 1982).

Servin, James, 'Chic or Cruel?', *New York Times*, 1 November 1992, Section 9 Signs of the *Times*, p. 1.

'£17m in Sales ... and More to Come', *Daily Mail*, 13 July 1976, n. p.

Shakespeare, R. W., 'Return of a Cult', *Stage and Television Today*, 11 November 1976, p. 22.

Shapiro, Mitchell E., *Television Network Prime-Time Programming, 1948–1988* (Jefferson: McFarland and Company, 1989).

Short, Don, 'The Ultimate Avenger: Stand By for Britain's New Saviour', *Sunday Mirror*, 3 October 1976, pp. 10–11.

Shulman, Milton, 'Sold Abroad: The Celluloid Hero', *Evening Standard*, 1 December 1965, n. p.

Skin Two Wetzine. no. 25, 1996, http://www.skintwo.co.uk

Smith, Ronald L., *Sweethearts of '60s TV: The Dream Wives, Girls Next Door, Comic Cuties, Women of Action, and Fantasy Figures from Your Favorite Shows* (New York: St Martin's Press, 1989).

Solomon, Harvey, 'Before Mrs Peel, there was ... An Avenger to Remember', *TV Guide*, vol. 38, no. 40, 6 October 1990, p. 15.

Sontag, Susan, *Against Interpretation and Other Essays* (New York: Delta, 1979).

Spindler, Amy M., 'Review/Fashion: Chanel's Message: Dress to Seduce', *New York Times*, 18 October 1994, Section B Style Desk, p. 13.

—— 'When Clothes Become You', *New York Times*, 22 September 1996, Section 6 Part 2 p. 36.

Stafford, David A. T., 'Spies and Gentlemen: The Birth of the British Spy Novel, 1893–1914', *Victorian Studies*, vol. 24, no. 4, 1981, pp. 489–509.

'Star Tracks', *People*, vol. 45, no. 14, 2 October 1995, p. 8.

Stern, Matthew Morgen, 'The Marshall Chronicles', *Primetime*, no. 13, winter 1987–8, pp. 2–7.

Steyn, Mark, *Mail on Sunday*, 14 February 1993, p. 53.

Sutcliffe, Kevin, 'Making a Killing: Interview with Brian Clemens', *Primetime*, no. 8, spring 1984, pp. 29–31.

Swallow, James, 'American Skeptic', *Starlog Science-Fiction Explorer*, no. 11, February 1996, pp. 12–15.

Sweeting, Adam, 'Back with a Vengeance', *Guardian*, 16 October 1993, p. 26.

Tankel, Jonathan David, 'Program Production for Export and the Domestic Market: Authorship in *The Avengers*', in Robert J. Thompson and Gary Burns (eds), *Making Television: Authorship and the Production Process* (New York: Praeger, 1990), pp. 81–91.

Tarpey, Mary, 'Your View', *Evening News*, 10 November 1977, n. p.

Taylor, Dorothea, 'The Proposal Diana Rigg Couldn't Turn Down: "Marry Me – Or Else!"', *Modern Screen*, February 1974, pp. 43–4, 64, 68.

Taylor, John, 'Colour T.V. Will Make Peacocks of Us All', *Men Only*, March 1968, pp. 60–1.

— 'Dressing Up for a Life of Crime', *Men Only*, June 1968, pp. 52–5.

Teranko, 'News and Notes From Nick Fury's Alter Ego', *En Garde*, no. 6, 1969, pp. 83–101.

Terrace, Vincent, *Television Character and Story Facts: Over 110,000 Details from 1,008 Shows, 1945–1992* (Jefferson: McFarland and Company, 1993).

Thomas, David, *Sunday Express*, 12 February 1995, p. 60.

Thomas, James, 'Steed Got the Champagne, but Apollo Earned all the Glory', *Daily Express*, 14 May 1969, n. p.

Thomas, Lyn, 'In Love with *Inspector Morse*: Feminist Subculture and Quality Television', *Feminist Review*, no. 51, autumn 1995, pp. 1–25.

Thorburn, David, 'Television Melodrama', in Horace Newcomb (ed.), *Television: The Critical View*, 2nd edn (New York: Oxford University Press, 1979), pp. 536–53.

Thorson, Linda, 'La Chance de Ma Vie', trans. Bruno Billion, in Alain Carrazé and Jean-Luc Putheaud, *Chapeau, Melon et Bottes de Cuir* (Paris: Huitième Art, 1990), pp. 18–20.

Toniello, Florent, *Avengers Home Page*. http://www.univ-lille 1.fr/~dessrc2/florent/avengers.html

The Trials and Tribulations of Emma Peel. http://www.tripciacy. demon.co.uk/avengers.htm

Tuchman, Gaye, 'Women's Depiction by the Mass Media', *Signs: Journal of Women in Culture and Society*, vol. 4, no. 3, 1979, pp. 528–42.

Tulloch, John and Manuel Alvarado, '*Doctor Who*': *The Unfolding Text* (New York: St Martin's Press, 1983).

Tulloch, John and Henry Jenkins, *Science Fiction Audiences: Watching 'Doctor Who' and 'Star Trek'* (London: Routledge, 1995).

Tulloch, Lee, *Fabulous Nobodies* (London: Chatto and Windus, 1989).

Twentieth Century Fund Task Force on Public Television, *Quality Time?* (New York: Twentieth Century Fund Press, 1993).

Usher, Shaun, 'The Mail TV Critic', *Daily Mail*, 20 October 1976, n. p.

Vincent-Rudzki, Jan, 'Brian Clemens: Writer, Creator, Producer . . .', *TV Zone*, no. 28, n. d, pp. 9–11.

Wark, Wesley K., 'The Intelligence Revolution and the Future', *Queen's Quarterly*, vol. 100, no. 2, summer 1993, pp. 273–87.

Weinberg, Martin S., Colin J. Williams and Cassandra Calhan, '"If the Shoe Fits . . ."; Exploring Male Homosexual Foot Fetishism', *Journal of Sex Research*, vol. 32, no. 1, 1995, pp. 17–27.

Westlake, Mike, 'The Classic TV Detective Genre', *Framework*, no. 13, 1980, pp. 37–8.

'What is an AVENGERS Fanatic?', *With Macintosh, Life Saver & Hard Hat*, 1985, p. 3.

Wheelwright, Julie, 'Poisoned Honey: The Myth of Women in Espionage', *Queen's Quarterly*, vol. 100, no. 2, summer 1993, pp. 290–309.

Wiggin, Maurice, 'Television', *Sunday Times*, 3 October 1965, n. p.

Willemen, Paul and Noel King, 'Through the Glass Darkly: Cinephilia Reconsidered', in Paul Willemen, *Looks and Frictions: Essays in Cultural Studies and Film Theory* (Bloomington: Indiana University Press, 1994), pp. 223–57.

Williams, Martin, *TV: The Casual Art* (New York: Oxford University Press, 1982).

Williams, Raymond, *Raymond Williams on Television: Selected Writings*, ed. Alan O'Connor (London: Routledge, 1989).

Williams, Scott, 'The Real Avenger', *Los Angeles Times*, 1992, p. 15.

Wilson, Jonathan, 'Back with Avengers', *Observer*, 24 October 1993, pp. 8–9.

Wilson, Simon, *Pop* (London: Thames and Hudson, 1974).

Winckler, Martin, 'Chapeau, Melon et Bottes de Cuir Alias "The Avengers" ', *Génération Séries*, no. 12, winter 1995, pp. 8–11.

With Umbrella, Charm & Bowler, vol. 2, no. 8, September 1984 and vol. 2, no. 9, 1985.

Worpole, Ken, *Reading By Numbers: Contemporary Publishing and Popular Fiction* (London: Comedia Publishing, 1984).

'WTVA', *Primetime*, vol. 1, no. 1, 1981, n. p.

Youlden, Richard, 'Avenging Angels', *What Satellite TV*, April 1994, pp. 57–61.

Yule, Andrew, *Sean Connery: From 007 to Hollywood Icon* (New York: Pinnacle Books, 1992).

Selected Credits

(Sources: Rogers *Complete*; Cornell, Day and Topping *The Avengers*)

The Avengers 161 episodes x 50 minutes
Produced at Associated British Studios by Associated British
Pictures Corporation. World distribution by Associated British
Pathé.

Seasons
Hendry–Macnee: 7 January to 30 December 1961, 26 black-and-white episodes

Macnee–Blackman: 29 September 1962 to 23 March 1963, 26 black-and-white episodes

Macnee–Blackman: 28 September 1963 to 21 March 1964, 26 black-and-white episodes

Macnee–Rigg: 2 October 1965 to 26 March 1966, 26 black-and-white episodes

Macnee–Rigg: 14 January 1967 to 18 November 1967, 24 colour episodes.

Macnee–Thorson: 25 September 1968 to 21 May 1969, 33 colour episodes

Vehicles
Steed:
Bugatti GK 3295: Vauxhall 30-98 XT 2273; Trojan Bubblecar CMU
574A; bicycle; yellow 1927 Rolls-Royce KK 4976; yellow 1923
Rolls-Royce Phantom UU 3864; dark-green 4.5 litre Bentley 1926
and 1927 UW 4887 and YT 3942; green 1926 Speed Six Bentley RX
6180; green 1928 Bentley YK 6871; green Range Rover WX 887.

Gale:
Triumph; motor cycle 987 CAA

Peel:
Powder-blue 1966 Lotus Elan HNK 999C and SJH 499C

King:
Red Lotus Europa PPW 999F; maroon AC Cobra LPH 800D; Mini Moke LYP 794D

Cast
Ian Hendry (David Keel), Patrick Macnee (John Steed), Honor Blackman (Catherine Gale), Julie Stevens (Venus Smith), Jon Rollason (Martin King), Diana Rigg (Emma Peel), Linda Thorson (Tara King), Douglas Muir (One-Ten), Paul Whitsun Jones (Charles), Ronald Radd (Quilpie), Patrick Newell (Mother), Ingrid Hafner (Carol Wilson), Arthur Hewlett (One-Twelve)
Ensemble actors in the series included the following notables:
Charlotte Rampling, Donald Sutherland, Fulton Mackay, Cecil Parker, Arthur Lowe, Valentine Dyall, Dennis Price, Frank Windsor, Christopher Lee, Roy Kinnear, Bernard Cribbins, Freddie Jones, Stratford Johns, Ronnie Barker, Patrick Cargill, Peter Cushing, Moira Lister, Lois Maxwell, Ron Moody, Brian Blessed, Philip Locke, Nigel Stock, John le Mesurier, Gerald Harper, Peter Jones, Nigel Davenport, Peter Wyngarde, Jon Pertwee, Anthony Valentine, Yootha Joyce, Clive Dunn, Penelope Keith, William Franklyn, Fenella Fielding, John Thaw, Corin Redgrave, Steven Berkoff, Ronald Fraser, Gordon Jackson, Warren Mitchell, John Cleese, Paul Eddington, Ray Barrett, Charles Tingwell, Peter Barkworth, Allan Cuthbertson, Leonard Rossiter, John Junkin, Judy Parfitt, T.P. McKenna, Andrew Keir, Edward Fox, Peter Bowles, Nyree Dawn Porter

Designers
Paul Bernard, Stephen Doncaster, Patrick Downing, James Goddard, Terry Green, Philip Harrison, Douglas James, Robert Jones, Robert Macgowan, David Marshall, Alpho O'Reilly, Maurice Pelling, Harry Pottle, Wilfrid Shingleton, Anne Spavin, Voytek

Directors
Jonathan Alwyn, Robert Asher, Ray Austin, Bill Bain, Roy Baker, Laurence Bourne, Don Chaffey, Charles Crichton, Robert Day, Paul Dickson, Peter Duffell, Gordon Flemyng, Cyril Frankel, Robert Fuest, Peter Hammond, Richmond Harding, Sidney Hayers, James Hill, John Hough, Roger Jenkins, John Knight, John Krish, Quentin Lawrence, Don Leaver, Raymond Menmuir, Kim Mills, John Moxey, Leslie Norman, Gerry O'Hara, Cliff Owen, Roy Rossotti, Peter Graham Scott, Don Sharp, Peter Sykes, Robert Tronson, Dennis Vance, Guy Verney

Music
Johnny Dankworth, Laurie Johnson

Producers
John Bryce, Brian Clemens, Albert Fennell, Sydney Newman, Gordon L.T. Scott, Leonard White, Julian Wintle

Writers
Geoffrey Bellman, Brandon Brady, Jeremy Burnham, Patrick Campbell, Philip Chambers, Brian Clemens, Lewis Davidson, Reed R. De Rouen, Terence Dicks, Fred Edge, Rex Edwards, Terence Feely, Colin Finbow, Leonard Fincham, Dave Freeman, John Gilbert, Richard Harris, Malcolm Hulke, Donald James, John Kruse, Philip Levene, Peter Ling, John Lucarotti, Richard Lucas, Max Marquis, Roger Marshall, Berkley Mather, James Mitchell, Doreen Montgomery, Terry Nation, Phyllis Norman, Geoffrey Orme, Eric Paice, Ludovic Peters, Lester Powell, Edward Rhodes, Ray Rigby, Jeremy Scott, Bryan Sherriff, Dennis Spooner, Robert Banks Stewart, Bill Strutton, Anthony Terpiloff, Leigh Vance, Gerald Verner, Sheilagh Ward, Jon Manchip White, John Whitney, Tony Williamson, Michael Winder, Martin Woodhouse

New Avengers 26 episodes x 50 minutes

Produced by Avengers (Film & TV) Enterprises Ltd, IDTV TV Productions, and Neilsen-Ferns

Seasons
Macnee–Lumley–Hunt: 22 October 1976 to 27 January 1977, 13 colour episodes

Macnee–Lumley–Hunt: 21 October 1977 to 1 December 1977, 13 colour episodes

Vehicles
Steed:
Olive-green 5.3 litre Jaguar Coupé NVK 60P; yellow River saloon WOC 229P; green Range Rover TXC 922J

Purdey:
Yellow MGB Sport MOC 232P; red Honda motor bike OLR 471P; yellow Triumph TR7 OGW 562R; yellow Honda LLC 950P

Gambit:
Red Jaguar MLR 875P; white Range Rover LOK 537P

Cast
Patrick Macnee (John Steed), Joanna Lumley (Purdey), Gareth Hunt (Gambit)
Ensemble actors included: Lewis Collins, Peter Cushing, Ed Devereaux, Jon Finch, William Franklyn, Barry Jackson, Jo Kendall, Peter Porteous, Clive Revill, Martin Shaw

Designers
Daniel Budin, Syd Cain, Seamus Flannery

Directors
Ray Austin, Graeme Clifford, Yvon Marie Coulais, Desmond Davis, Ernest Day, George Fournier, Robert Fuest, Richard Gilbert, Sidney Hayers, James Hill, John Hough, Don Thompson

SELECTED CREDITS

Music
Laurie Johnson

Producers
Brian Clemens, Albert Fennell

Writers
Brian Clemens, Terence Feely, John Goldsmith, Dennis Spooner

Index